The Final Imperative

An Islamic Theology of Liberation

By the same author

BE CAREFUL WITH MUHAMMAD!
The Salman Rushdie Affair

A FAITH FOR ALL SEASONS
Islam and Western Modernity

THE FINAL IMPERATIVE

An Islamic Theology of Liberation

Shabbir Akhtar

Bellew Publishing
London

BP
170
.A378
1991

*To the memory of Khalid al-Islambuli and
Abdal-Salam Faraj, martyrs for the Islamic cause,
living and rejoicing in God's provision.*

First published in Great Britain in 1991 by
Bellew Publishing Company Limited
7 Southampton Place
London
WC1A 2DR

Copyright © Shabbir Akhtar 1991

ISBN 0 947792 93 7

Phototypeset by Intype, London
Printed and bound in Great Britain by
Billings & Sons Ltd

This book is sold subject to the condition that it
shall not, by way of trade or otherwise, be lent, re-sold,
hired out, or otherwise circulated without the
Publisher's prior consent in any form of binding or
cover other than that in which it is published and
without a similar condition including this condition
being imposed on the subsequent purchaser. This book
is published at a net price and is supplied subject to
the Publishers Association Standard Conditions of Sale
registered under the Restrictive Trade Practices Act, 1956.

Contents

Preface

Then the Devil took Jesus to a very high mountain and showed him all the kingdoms of the world in all their greatness. 'All this I will give you,' the Devil said, 'if you kneel down and worship me.'

So reads St Matthew's Gospel (4:8–9) on Christ's third temptation in the wilderness. Jesus' alleged repudiation of the political wing has had permanent consequences for any distinctively Christian reflection on power and polity. 'The Scripture says,' retorts Christ, 'Worship the Lord your God, and serve only Him!' (How *Islamic* an answer, incidentally.)

The purpose of this book is to explore the relationship between theological truth and secular power, and attain the right equilibrium between preaching and activism, the pen and the sword. What is, for the man of God, the correct attitude towards worldly powers and principalities? Christians and Muslims have responded differently here because Jesus of Nazareth and Muhammad of Mecca are thought to have given opposed verdicts. Their answers, in turn, have reflected and sustained differing portraits of the moral nature of deity.

The Arabian Prophet, of course, preached to the hostile pagan establishment of Mecca; after thirteen years he was expelled from the metropolis. After his emigration/exodus (*Hijra*) to Medina, he embraced the political arm, empowered his religion, and eventually conquered the entire power structure that had resisted his revolutionary proposals. He re-entered Mecca, in bloodless triumph, purified its precincts of all pagan association, and declared it the hub of the Muslim universe. And so it has remained up to this day.

Modern Christian apology has rigidly maintained that the adoption of the political course is a short-cut to the messianic goal – one which effectively compromises with evil. Jesus declined the choice of moving, so to speak, to his Medina, as a way out of the deadlock with the antagonistic establishment. In this way, Jesus resisted, while Muhammad succumbed, to the temptation to 'effect a detour', an alternative route requiring the sanction of force. In drinking from the cup of suffering, Christ opted for, in the Reverend Kenneth Cragg's words, 'the quiet strength of truth and the sure fidelities of love' (*Jesus and the Muslim*, London: George Allen and Unwin, 1985, p. 154).

In this book I examine and defend – against Christian and associated liberal accusation – the Muslim stance on the status of worldly power. It is an apt time to do so. Under the impact of increasing tensions in the Muslim world in the last two decades there has been an attempt, quite deliberate and perhaps even co-ordinated, to construct an influential stereotype of contemporary 'fundamentalist' Islam as a violent creed. The stereotype feeds on indelible images of apparently motiveless malice and terror; Islam and all things Islamic are these days synonymous with a fanatical bloodthirstiness sustained by and in turn sustaining an overwhelming lust for power. In such a context, the Muslim frankness about the morality of constraint often leads Christians to accuse Muslims of being unscrupulous warmongers.

I explore and defend the traditional Muslim confidence that 'political religion', for want of a better phrase, is the only alternative to daydreaming. Also contained here is the conceptual framework for a complete 'Muslim liberation theology'. My aim is primarily to sketch the terrain; but I do not pretend to any neutrality on the large and practical questions of the legitimacy of political violence in the contemporary scene. My account implies distinctively Muslim verdicts about establishments and militancies in places and consciences as diverse as Latin America, Israel's occupied territories, South Africa, Brazil, Northern Ireland and other troubled lands. Islam, unlike a religion such as Buddhism – if indeed one can call it a religion and not merely, in Nietzsche's phrase, 'spiritual hygiene' – takes its political obligations very seriously. Accordingly, as a Muslim scholar, I continually imply political judgements. It is every Muslim believer's duty to identify injustice and to call it by its name. Wherever religious obligation and the demands of professional detachment have clashed, I have not hesitated about which loyalty comes first.

SHABBIR AKHTAR
Bradford, 1991

Introduction: A New World Order?

1

In October 1981, in full view of the television cameras, a military truck suddenly stopped during a parade in honour of Egypt's President Anwar Sadat. Four men stepped down and opened fire with automatic weapons at the review stand. Sadat was killed. The leader of the attackers was a young Lieutenant called Khalid al-Islambouli who belonged to the outlawed *jihād* movement.

It was the courageous al-Islambouli who seized the head-lines. But the *jihād* movement owed its ideas to a certain Abdal-Salam Faraj who had just published an iconoclastic work, *The Mysterious Obligation (al-Farda al-Ghayyiba)*, which established him as the foremost militant Muslim intellectual in his country. Faraj's predecessors, notably Shukri Mustafa, had believed that Egyptian society was un-Islamic principally because it was ruled by a secular system of government. Faraj, taking his cue from the great medieval thinker, ibn Taimiyya, argued that most modern Egyptians are Muslim believers but their rulers are disbe-lievers because they reject Islamic law. Today, as in the days of the Mongol rule of Islamic lands, Islam has been reduced to an item of piety in the private sector: 'today's rulers are apostates . . . All they preserve of Islam is its name.'

Ibn Taimiyya's major work on the sacred law (*Shari'ah*) had been an attempt to explore in detail the obligation to engage in holy struggle against militant evil. There is nothing new about the endorsement of *jihād* – often inter-preted to be the sixth pillar of Islam after the five canonical articles of faith. But ibn Taimiyya went further in reviving the potentially revolutionary suggestion of the early Shafi'i

1

jurist, al-Mazini, that there can validly be a *jihād within* the community of Islam. Where ostensibly Muslim sultans and kings behave unjustly or seek to secularize the Islamic power structure, it is incumbent upon their Muslim subjects to rise up against them.

The contemporary Egyptian scene is politically messy. It is the battleground of rival Islamic factions vying for power and the stamp of authentic radicalism. Members of the *jihād* movement condemn the older Muslim Brotherhood, founded by al-Banna and Sayyid Quṭb, as having partly compromised with the establishment. Some of the Brothers have recently opted for gradual reform through the existing secular structures rather than revolution and a purist attachment to Islam as a totally exclusive ideology. The Brotherhood has therefore attained some official recognition in Parliament while all the *jihād* radicals continue to languish in prison. Al-Islambouli and Faraj were both executed.

An examination of the life and vision of the founders of the Muslim Brotherhood is given in Chapter 5. Here it only remains to add that the man who issued a *fatwa* authorizing the assassination of Sadat is still alive. He is Sheikh Umar Abdal Rahman, a blind preacher living in the city of Fayoum, teaching at one of the al-Azhar colleges for girls, and intermittently under house arrest. Six months before his assassination, Sadat had, during a live televised debate in the al-Azhar seminary, trampled on the cap of his Muslim protagonist. As early as 1961, in an attempt to reduce the independence and enthusiasm of Islamic religionists, Jamal Abdal Nasser had nationalized al-Azhar. Yet despite that, even a symbolic attack on the authority of the Muslim scholars was not allowed to go unpunished.

2

There is, if unintentionally, something new about the New World Order: Islam. At the end of the nineteenth century, Islam was everywhere a defeated, dying, tamed, spent force. The European colonialists were celebrating. At the close of the twentieth century, Islam has re-emerged as a genuinely radical, indeed wholly unmanageable, ideology that proudly takes its place as a major player on the international political stage. With the universal decline of Communism and the manifest failure of foreign imports – pan-Arabism, Arab nationalism, Arab socialism – Islam, the indigenous faith, has returned to plague the labours of its enemies. The radicalization of the Muslim peoples is a standing item on every western and secular Arab agenda. The storms that now blow across Arab deserts can dethrone kings.

In Europe, Islam is a player in the politics of difference. The Muslims, expelled forcibly from Spain and Europe about five hundred years ago, have returned. But this is no return of the barbarians. Their new peaceful presence in Europe is part of an experiment in multi-cultural citizenship. After the Rushdie furore, Muslims have become Europeans; Islam is no longer an alien Semitic force out there in some exotic land.

More narrowly, British Muslims have launched an Islamic Party as an alternative to the major power groupings. The attempt may be premature and unsuccessful, but that there should be such an attempt at all is politically significant. To those who fear Islam while pretending to despise it, the endeavour is simply a confirmation of the evident impudence of a minority that behaves like a majority – an attitude that is, ironically, also characteristic of white settlers in their enduring colonial scramble for Africa, Asia, Latin America and the Middle East. That Muslim behaviour should puncture the arrogance of certain individuals and ruling establishments in the West is hardly surprising. To Muslims and their few sympathizers, however, the Islamic attempt to enter the political arena is seen as being inspired by an instinctive recognition of the irreducible risks of powerlessness.

Western experts often claim that democracy cannot blossom on Muslim soil because Islam as a revealed religion is naturally authoritarian, indeed Fascist. This is a view which

3

has, in that American colloquialism, everything going for it except the evidence. Much of the current opposition to democracy in Islamic lands comes directly from Western government policy rather than from the activities of those omnipresent villains, the Muslim fundamentalists.

Several repressive regimes in the Islamic world are actively supported by Western powers, particularly the USA, Britain and France. The CIA continues to help many a tyrant. The Americans and the British befriended the Shah of Iran. Saddam Hussein was a friend of the democratic West until he raped Kuwait and his Western admirers decided to revise their definitions of good and evil. The French have encouraged many pro-Western dictatorships in North Africa. There are only dependent and independent dictatorships in the House of Islam; and the West supports the dependent ones. Is it, then, in the interests of Western powers even to allow, let alone encourage, democracy on Islamic soil?

The legitimate desire of Muslim peoples to shape their societies, to control their resources, has long been hampered by outside powers who resent the inconvenience that much of the world's oil is under Arab and Iranian soil. (The discovery of North Sea oil was almost a religious event in Britain: it was a relief to know that God wasn't a Muslim!) Britain, France, and the US have always singled out a few Muslim rulers for special protection, ensuring their prosperity and absolute power usually at the expense of their people. The result is a few spectacularly rich Sheikhs engaged in vulgar displays of wealth and sexual prowess, providing material for our tabloids.

In their own countries and in lands where they have no wish to control others' destinies, Westerners are genuinely fair-minded, thoughtful and restrained. It is only in other peoples' lands that Westerners behave unjustly and arrogantly. 'Do in Rome as the Romans do' is not a proverb any Englishman takes seriously. This moral schizophrenia, crudely called 'double standards', is actually a disease in the soul; its symptoms include the Gulf tragedy and the poison of Northern Ireland.

We Muslims rightly resent the West's interference in Islamic affairs, its determined attempts to place Westerners and their fellow 'Muslim' conspirators at the helm of our political destinies. Britain and America have no right to arrange peace conferences to decide our fate: the House of Islam is not an American protectorate.

3

An English friend recently asked me: 'Did you resent a woman Prime Minister of Pakistan, an Islamic country?' 'No,' I said, 'but I do resent a disbeliever ruling a Muslim land.' Benazir Bhutto's autobiography *Daughter of the East* is actually the story of a typical daughter of the West.

During the '80s, there has been a recognizable move towards democracy in several Islamic lands, including Algeria, Jordan and Iran – possibly the most mature democracy in the contemporary Islamic world. But the move has been predictably opposed both by Western governments and by 'brown sahibs' – the indigenous Westernized élite who inherited colonial rule of the Muslim peoples. Despite such opposition, Muslim populations are increasingly using the ballot-box to place their trust in Muslim leaders who sympathize with Islamic ideals. Algeria is an outstanding example. The Muslim fundamentalists there have peacefully acquired power and are using it to implement the wishes of the majority. In 1990, Algerian legislators received popular requests for an approval of the revolutionary law of 'total return to Arab culture' (*al-Quanun at-Tartib Ash-Shamil*).

Pakistan is currently in the throes of a genuine struggle between the élite rulers who oppose Islam as a piece of outdated superstition and their Muslim constituency which largely welcomes it as a vital part of its identity. In 1991, Pakistan's Parliament voted to adopt Islamic Law (*Shari'ah*) as supreme. The Senate passed the controversial legislation after rejecting the forty Opposition amendments falsely denouncing the Shari'ah Bill as an undemocratic ordinance.

None of these developments in Islamic lands is surprising. The basic Islamic tenet of consultation (*shura*) among believers is essentially a democratic principle. Western experts have dishonestly denied the democratic potential of Islam just as they have naively promoted the myth of a democratic, non-violent and secular India. In the former case, hatred and fear are the motives; in the latter, nostalgia and sentimentality. None can lead to truth.

This is not to deny that Muslims have much to learn from Western models of democracy. Islamic society still needs to build mechanisms for appointing, maintaining, and removing political leadership in a safe, just and preferably peaceful manner. Assassination remains a normal liability of political life in all Third World countries.

As the Pakistani case shows, the question of multi-party politics in Islam still remains intractable. Traditional Islam discourages this style of managing a community's political differences. The ancient Muslim thinkers saw the issue concerning choice between rival parties as important but not fundamental. (In modern Britain, this question is relatively unimportant for most citizens and wholly trivial for Muslims.) The deeper problem is the attempt to make political authority accountable to an electorate, Muslim or otherwise, and to raise the routine professions of political humility to something above the level of slogans and rhetoric.

It is an open question whether or not Islam endorses some pattern of government that bears a family resemblance to democracy. For democracy is itself an essentially contested concept. The struggle to define it in a particular way is itself part of a political, not purely theoretical, endeavour. The term 'democracy' has now acquired an approbative force that all parties to the dispute wish to annex. 'Theocracy' is, by contrast, a dirty word: it is best seen as a form of government inspired by an innocent variety of extreme arrogance. It is part of my task to dispute this verdict as unempirical and unfair.

4

Some tired and irate voice says: 'At the end of the chapter, politics must tolerate the evil that power brings in its train.' Must it? Why not: 'Politics must eradicate the kind of evil that power instigates'? There cannot be a more precise way of putting the elemental rift between a Christian vision in which the world is politically fallen and an Islamic one in which the world can surely be redeemed partly via the political. I explore and assess the tangled skein of reasoning here through a detailed examination of the work of the Anglican Arabist, Kenneth Cragg.

Of course, the mandate for peace is everywhere plentiful. Daily life, history, religion and secular ethics are not the only advocates. But we Muslims never asked for an easy peace that has compromised with evil and injustice. The ancient voice of Jeremiah wistfully pleads for peace often enough – too often in its own setting knowing that, in those days, God was young and virile. Yet, elsewhere, the peace-loving visionary himself laments: 'We looked for peace, but no good came' (Jeremiah, 8:15). Many today pretend to be looking for peace – and much evil comes of it. In their case, what I say here may be convicted of lacking in diplomacy and restraint; it will not be accused of lacking in frankness or sincerity.

There is only one further issue left, elemental and native and therefore entitled to the last word. Our pursuit of power is instinctive. Nor is this restricted to the arena of our social dealings as citizens. Something as private as romantic love can have political significance. Even between two persons there can be a relationship of power, characterized by control and force. Loving can be a political act at least in an individual if not social sense: it revolutionizes at least one's own world. 'All is fair in love and war' is a morally questionable maxim but it is right in seeing both love and war as being implicated in interpersonal power. The aim of a decisive religion is to ensure that love does not lapse into tyranny anywhere in life and that Caesar does not usurp what belongs to God.

1   The Bible in One Hand . . .

The neo-orthodox theologian Karl Barth used to quip that he read the Bible in one hand and a newspaper in the other. Suppose that all religious believers, including Christians and Muslims, adopted his style of reading. What would they find in the Bible or the Koran – and in the newspaper? Is sacred literature relevant to contemporary global concerns of social injustice, poverty, unemployment and violence? Which of the texts – the sacred or the fallible – should set the agenda for our modern anguish? Should one read the biblical and koranic imperatives 'into' the headlines? Or should the headlines be read backwards into the eternal books of God? Is scripture the record of God's dealings with men and women? Are our dealings with each other the necessary context for God's plan for liberating the oppressed through the appointment of Moses and Muhammad?

Such worries must have exercised several Christian thinkers at the Medellin Conference, held in Colombia in 1968. Described as the Vatican II of Latin America, theologians there had raised disturbing questions about the proper Christian response to the marginalization of a vast segment of the human race condemned to live in perpetual poverty and degradation. The issues were all the more pressing since this unacceptable state of affairs was initially inaugurated and subsequently perpetuated by prosperous Western Christian nations. The cross and the sword had been constant companions in the vast historical enterprise of occidental aggression. Injustice was indeed, the theologians conceded, a scandalous condition that must be remedied: it injured human dignity and was therefore necessarily contrary to the will of the Christian God. It was concluded that the oppressors would at best give charity, not justice; the poor wanted justice, not charity.

In 1973, the Peruvian theologian Gustavo Gutiérrez clinched the case. His *A Theology of Liberation*, published in that year, is an outstanding work. It proved to be an influential manifesto, inspiring and guiding a major theological initiative in twentieth-century Christianity. Gutiérrez argued that liberation from the personal prison of sin is incomplete without the further liberation from unjust human structures of power. And to effect a distinction between the political and the religious is already a political act. In any case, private salvation seems futile in a world of public distress.

Liberation theologians characteristically emphasize the need to liberate oneself and others from all forms of oppression – the private burden of sin, of course, but also public forms of bondage: political, economic, racial, sexual, environmental and even 'religious'. In Latin American contexts, the concern has primarily settled on the shocking level of political and economic repression of poverty-stricken masses; in South Africa it has been, predictably, the attempt to question the white ruling élite's brutal suppression of black human rights; in South Asia, the problem of eradicating spectacular poverty has attracted the theologian's attention.

Liberation theology is founded on the conviction that God is capable of suffering. (How strange that Christian orthodoxy, itself inspired by the sight of a crucified Lord, could ever have held otherwise!) The Christian deity, as a suffering God, naturally has sympathy for those human beings who also suffer. The liberation theologian ponders and meditates not in the detached setting of academia, but rather in the hurly-burly of ordinary life: his theology is, therefore, spontaneously generated at grass (or rice)-roots level, inspired as it is by a direct knowledge, even experience, of the deprivations and tribulations of small, poor minorities professing the Gospel in the face of callous witness.

This religious movement has been dubbed 'poor the-

ology'. It is an appropriately vague term that can be used
descriptively, approvingly, or else pejoratively. It could be
interpreted to mean a religious programme of liberating
the powerless and rightless masses of the Third World by
exercising a 'preferential option for the poor'. Alternatively, critics dismiss it as a theology that is unorthodox and
inadequate, unfaithful to the unarmed Christ's teachings, a
heretical theology that effectively baptizes socialism and
legitimizes the use of force in political struggle.

The standard indictment of liberation theology by orthodox Christian writers is remarkably similar in status and
motivation to their indictment of the Islamic involvement
with power. (Could this be because liberation theology is
effectively an Islamization of Christianity?) Conversely,
the rejoinders of liberation theologians to their orthodox
co-religionists bear a striking resemblance to the standard
Islamic critique of official Christianity's alleged withdrawal
from the political sector.

Let us look at each in turn. The central accusation is
that the hero of liberation theology is not Jesus of Gethsemane but rather a political activist resembling Judas Maccabaeus, or, one might add, Muhammad of Medina. Liberation theology, the accusation continues, devalues religious
reflection while exalting political action. Traditional Christianity, it is concluded, is reduced merely to a form of
secular idealism, a Christian-sounding appendix to a declaration of human rights.

But what is the point of religious meditation if it fails
to affect our practical conduct or, worse, immobilizes us
completely? Equally, what is the purpose of a political
activism uninformed by religious scruple? Surely, we need
a balance between thought and action. And granted that
Christianity is not solely a declaration of the rights of Man,
is not all authentic theism minimally concerned to secure
these? Granted that one of the heroes of liberation theology is indeed a Judas Maccabaeus, why should Jesus'
(alleged) passivity in the face of evil be the *only* characteristically religious episode in his life and prophetic career?

The last point needs elaboration. Modern historical

research has been obliged to modify the traditional Gospel picture of a pacifist Jesus in order to countenance and explain events such as the forcible expulsion of the money-lenders from the Temple. This is not the place to speculate about the exact relationship between Jesus and members of the Essene community, who were certainly not averse to the use of force. But it is fair to state that both Christian and non-Christian historians, notably the renowned Jewish scholar Geza Vermes, have given all orthodox Christians second thoughts about the received portrait of the histori-cal Jesus. The great prophet has been steadily Judaized and, by parallel implication, Islamicized, in recent decades. He emerges as a charismatic reformer concerned to pose an active challenge to those institutions and individuals who degrade the powerless and dispossessed.

Recent cases of irresponsible Christian pacifism, especially as exemplified in the Church's firm refusal to sanction violent resistance to Hitler's régime, have led some Christian writers to revise the traditional Christian attitude to physical power. In his frank and original mono-graph *A Theology of Force and Violence* (London: SCM Press, 1989), Father Peter Mayhew speaks for a few fellow Christians when he claims that the use of force is some-times necessitated by the very intransigence of evil, that war is tragically often the only way to ensure a hearing for peace. Between the extremes of absolute principled pacifism and unconstructive, motiveless violence, there is the justifiable option of violent revolution for the sake of enduring peace and justice. Constructive violence, moti-vated by mercy rather than malice, can certainly be defended. (Indeed it has been thus defended in the 'just war' tradition of Catholic Christianity.) And, paradoxi-cally, virtually every modern democracy is founded on bloodshed.

Mayhew himself concludes that where injustice persists despite lengthy pacific protest, the pursuit of justice may sadly require the Christian conscience to endorse violent options. He believes that the pacifist interpretation of New Testament teaching ignores its equally forthright and more time-honoured emphasis on the need to secure social justice by confronting those forces of communal wrongdoing which usurp others' legitimate rights.

Mayhew's eloquent and moving voice is heard only in the Western wilderness. The prevalent post-medieval view about Christianity's proper rôle in the political realm is expressed historically by Martin Luther, and in our own day by the clergy of the established Church of England. There is, naturally, always the dissident voice. We have had John Calvin, who insisted that the Church of Christ should be a thorn in the secular flesh constantly piercing secular powers, forcing worldly rulers to know and acknowledge their limits and duties. And there is always the individual Christian militant who takes issue with official orthodoxy.

Luther's 'Two Kingdoms' approach, which effectively depoliticized Christianity, has proved to be remarkably influential, especially in Protestant denominations such as Anglicanism. The secular state is to be supreme in matters of this world. A Christian is to build an alternative kingdom that is not of this world – a kingdom created by withdrawing from the political arena in order to maintain a fellowship of love where compromises with power are necessarily out of the question. And never should the twain meet. The result is a mutually supportive relationship between the official faith and the political order that is associated with it: piety implies patriotism and, contingently, vice versa.

It is this close identification of institutional Christianity with capitalism and exploitative Western power structures that has excited the anger of liberation theologians. Their argument has been that authentic Christianity is far easier to practise in a socialist than in a capitalist economy. The kind of Christianity that flourishes in post-Thatcher Britain, for example, has been condemned as being opposed in spirit to the fundamental teachings of Jesus. And if this type of Western Christianity is treasonable to the cause of Christ, its effects on Third World segments of our common humanity are even more catastrophic. The Christian record is deplorable; Christians have far too readily besmirched the purity of Jesus' message. It is a standing reproof to Western Christians that they have failed to condemn effectively the aggressive behaviour of unjust settler minorities in countries such as Israel and South Africa.

It is not unfair to state that contemporary European and American Christians are content to confine their faith and its universal claims to a social ghetto from which it poses no threat to the political order. Christianity is an established faith, a religion that has been domesticated within an essentially upper- and middle-class domain. This truncated religion is appreciated and even applauded by the powerful secular establishment precisely because Christians humbly acknowledge their limits and rarely ask awkward questions that might awaken memories of that poor, derided, outcast, crucified God come to earth at the sight of human hubris. This post-Enlightenment Christianity, willingly confined to the private sphere of piety, silently legitimizes the established order which, in turn, regularly manipulates it for its own secular ends. (Think here of the Church of England's endorsement of the Gulf conflict as a justifiable cause as soon as the British Government had decided to attack Iraq in 1991.) Both in North America and Europe, official Christianity performs the functions of a civil religion, accepts a conservative rôle, and is generally right-wing. Faith has here won a Pyrrhic victory over the secular order.

This is particularly true of the established Church of England, variously described by cynics as the ruling party at prayer and the most profitable of Britain's nationalized industries. In later chapters, I examine in detail the work of one of the leading Anglican thinkers of this century, the Rev. Kenneth Cragg, who takes Muslims to task for their embrace of the political arm. This is not the place to indulge the love of controversy for its own sake or to level accusations of double standards. It is sufficient to note here that another Anglican churchman, Dr John Habgood, in his *Church and Nation in a Secular Age* (London: Darton, Longman and Todd, 1983), does not offer a single theological, let alone Christian theological, argument for 'establishing' a Church. The contentions are all secular, pragmatic and broadly opportunistic: an established Church can be a force for moral good in a secular culture. Fair enough. But could there be any specifically Christian reason for refusing to confront a dominant modern secularity that daily encroaches on the traditional religious sanctities?

The truth is, of course, that 'establishment' compromises authentic religion. For establishment is effectively a secular technique for controlling the moral passion of supernatural faith, a way of curtailing its rôle as a potentially powerful force that might check the excesses of secular hubris, power and avarice. The Church of England, torn between its desire for worldly power and its professed vocation of powerlessness, has betrayed the mission of its Master, revealing to all how its Kingdom is very much of this world only. Christ, were he to return, would surely be more comfortable among the despised and impoverished British Muslims than the Anglicans, whose presence among the poor and deprived grows more tenuous by the day. Anglicanism, therefore, cannot be the establishment of the faith of Jesus and his disciples, but rather its manifest subversion. Whether or not such a Church should be disestablished in order to regain its integrity as genuinely Christian is a question I leave to the Anglican conscience. In the meantime, Muslims are entitled to remind Christians that worldly privilege and the cause of Christ are not natural allies, that the basic values of the Christian faith are not those of 'bourgeois' capitalism. Muslims certainly challenge the Western Christian Churches to become the custodians of God's word, not merely the nervous defenders of their own institutional interests.

The purpose of wedding religious restraint to political ambition is to see to it that, in the political field, the Devil does not have it all his own way – every day. At least on Sunday (or Friday), God is to be at the helm of our destiny as political creatures. 'Seek ye first the political kingdom' is no doubt an heretical imperative. But why not have the best of both worlds by seeking both kingdoms? And God is not the one to render vain our efforts.

2 A Tale of Two Cities

1

In the scorching summer of AD 622, a Jewish peasant from Medina spotted two weary travellers heading towards the shade of the palm trees. He recognized the two men to be Muhammad and his staunch ally Abū Bakr. He knew that having just escaped from Mecca they were seeking asylum in Medina. He did not know, however, that their arrival was to mark, for countless millions yet unborn, the beginning of a new era of world history.

The choice of AD 622 as the date for the inauguration of the Islamic era deserves comment. For a variety of reasons, both internal and external to Muslim confession, the choice of the event of the *Hijra* for originating the calendar is justified. To be sure, there is no shortage of pivotal and stirring occurrences in the early history of Islam which could arguably serve as points for dating. Why not choose the year 610, when the first koranic sequence was revealed? Why not the birth of the Prophet? Why not his death? Why not the decisive Battle of Badr?

Apart from a number of heretical mentalities – Libya's Colonel Qaddafi and the late deposed Shah of Iran for instance – no one has disputed the year 622 as the legitimate claimant for heading the Muslim calendar. There are multiple significances within the *Hijra* as, variously, the event that 'divides' the Koran, shifts the locus of the prophetic activity and transforms Islam from a tiny persecuted and powerless movement to a religious superpower in embryo. The event was in any case crucial to the whole future of the infant faith. An unarmed apostle who had taught the iconoclastic creed in Mecca naturally aroused

16

hostility; the impenitent city drove him out. Muhammad was willing to leave his native city – for the sake of that Lord and Master for whom he had sacrificed everything else. The decision to embark on the road to exile was not taken lightly; there are hints of pathos for the rejecting city in the opening verse of the *Sūra* entitled *'The City'*. But 'God is greater' – greater even than the love of one's birthplace.

The *Hijra* is among the most significant emigrations in the history of the human race. It proved to be an exemplary decision for the Muslim armies that, after the death of the Messenger, swept with ease beyond the Arabia of their origin into distant lands, east and west. Muslim warriors saw themselves as merely enlarging Muhammad's own witness to the greatness of God: hadn't the Apostle also left his native city for the sake of his Lord?

The *Hijra* has unsurprisingly remained, for Muslims ever since, a powerful symbol of the need for transcending local and national boundaries in the interests of a faith that is at once specific in its Arabian origin yet potentially global in its relevance. God is above patriotism. When the late Ayatollah Khomeini returned from exile to land on his native Iranian soil, a French journalist asked him how it felt. 'I feel nothing,' remarked the Ayatollah. Few non-Muslims, indeed even Muslims these days, can appreciate the meaning of his cryptic comment.

2

The event of the *Hijra* has excited significant critical comment, particularly from Christian quarters. It has been interpreted as a decisive politicization of faith, whereby Islam was permanently morally compromised. In his darkest hour, at the watershed of the prophetic career, the argument runs, Muhammad 'betrayed' his prophetic vocation. Unlike some other true servants of the Word, he opted for force and power – a change of policy reflected in the Koran's partial alteration of style from moral preaching to political and legal injunction.

The Christian reservation on this score has historically been associated with purely polemical intentions. The crudity of its traditional literature about its great rival is a sufficient witness to this. But in recent decades, the same reservation has been married to a considered and probing indictment of the traditional Islamic involvement with political power.

One of the ablest Christian students of Islam in this area of concern has been the Rev. Kenneth Cragg. In several works, particularly *Muhammad and the Christian* (London: Darton, Longman and Todd, 1984) and its companion volume *Jesus and the Muslim* (London: George Allen and Unwin, 1985), Cragg explores the theological grounds of a radical accusation. Are Muslims justified in placing confidence in the capacities of the state to deliver righteousness and justice in social policy? Was Muhammad right to recruit the political wing for the achievement of religious ends? Relying as it does on a multi-lingual scholarship and almost half a century of experience of Muslim involvement with power in the Middle Eastern context, Cragg's account should not be despised.

I shall explore the Islamic understanding of the correct relationship between power and truth and, in doing so, show that Cragg's critique begs important questions about the essence of original Islam as a unified enterprise of faith and power. Moreover, I believe it relies on a controversial if not mistaken conception of the 'political' dimension of the Muslim religion and indeed betrays a misunderstanding of the koranic perspective on failure in the political life and, more broadly, on the 'tragic' element in human life under divine sovereignty.

It would be disingenuous here to pretend that only Christians (or only their opponents) are in the grip of a vision. The issues are made almost intractable by the depth of loyalties that not only secrete criteria congenial to predetermined judgements but even exclude temporary suspensions of conviction for purposes of enquiry. Unsurprisingly, many doors are slammed over these matters in inter-faith gatherings. My procedure involves sustained argument

broken with the occasional hiatus in which I draw inferences about the central underlying issue here, namely,
the right relationship between theological truth and social
power. The very form of such a procedure encourages a
measure of detachment which, hopefully, reduces the risk
of bias.

Islam, as a specific historical faith, began in Mecca.
Owing to various historical complications, it first found
adequate political expression in Medina. Cragg's basic
charge is simple, and notwithstanding its apparent novelty,
is actually a refined version of a much older orientalist
thesis. Muhammad, it is claimed, betrayed his vocation.
In the hour of trial, at the moment of crisis – in the strict
sense of 'turning-point' – the undesirable Caesar in him
overwhelmed the gentler voice of God. Eager to see his
Lord and the cause of Islam victorious, the Arabian iconoclast sought a short-cut to triumph. But, argues Cragg, in
matters of the spirit, there exists neither a short-cut nor
any guarantee of success.

Cragg, like his Muslim opponents, sees the *Hijra* as a
pivotal event in the prophetic *sīra* (biography). The reasons
are of course different. Cragg interprets the *Hijra* event
to be the juncture where 'prophethood culminates and
rulership begins' (*Muhammad and the Christian*, p. 18).
What does this mean? We need to impose a reading on
this significant claim. I take it to mean that Muhammad's
tenure in the prophetic office came to an end – a climax,
if you like – while he was still in Mecca. At Medina, he
was no longer a genuine prophet but, one might say, a
kind of successor to that rôle – namely, a man concerned
to implement, with worldly means, the essentially religious
commission he had sincerely seen himself as receiving and
accepting in Mecca.

An auxiliary claim here buttresses this thesis. The message of God, according to Cragg, has no legitimate means
for its implementation in this world – except verbal exhortation, repeated enunciation, and trust in providence. The
decision to emigrate, the accusation continues, betrays an
unworthy desire for non-verbal means of success. But, we

are told, the Prophet's search for non-verbal means is a crucial indication of his impatience with the normal (and, for Cragg, only legitimate) arsenal available to those who are genuine prophets. Cragg quotes with approval the Koran's own claim that 'Thy task [i.e. Muhammad's] is merely to *convey* the message; it is for Us [i.e. God] to do *the reckoning* [*ḥisāb*], (Koran 13:40, emphasis added). The pagans didn't have to wait for God to do the reckoning. And that is Cragg's fundamental accusation. Muhammad's political activities in the post-*Hijra* years constitute betrayals, if unconscious and sincere, of that genuine spirituality so familiar to readers of the New Testament. For Cragg, Muhammad's *political* authority effectively negates his *religious* authority. For the Christian conscience reared on a diet of *agape* and forgiveness, willing to drink from the cup of suffering, ready to suffer willingly if unjustly, there is, Cragg concludes, 'an inescapable reservation of heart about the power dimension' (*Muhammad and the Christian*, p. 14) of the Arabian Prophet's Medinan ministry.

The messenger of God, then, has every right to take the wayward horse to water; but he has no right to make it drink. It was this essential limitation that, according to Cragg, both Muhammad and his Lord ignored. The Christian verdict must of necessity comment adversely on 'Muhammadan' and koranic militancy (*Muhammad and the Christian*, p. 23). There are specifically religious reasons for a prophet's resolute refusal to drink from the cup of power. The evil that rejects God and His ordinances, argues Cragg, merely withdraws deeper into the heart as political sanction chases it. In this way, men's hearts remain unconquered – within the province of a purely profane sovereignty. Hypocrisy becomes their refuge; the will to impiety is merely concealed from the public gaze. Yet God is well aware of it. The religious task, the argument continues, is to cauterize sin and perversity; and there is no political weapon that could do that. Secular power can build terrestrial empires but not spiritual ones. For it must necessarily fail to reach whole areas of

human existence and conviction, necessarily leave unfulfil-
led deep human needs and aspirations. Power cannot
accomplish love's task. And where it seems to succeed,
even there, in reality, it fails by generating contradiction
and compromise. For love has a range, depth, and capacity
unavailable to other facilities. The sword is no substitute
for the power of the message of love (*Jesus and the Muslim*,
p. 154).

3

Two remarks, related to the main thrust of this contention,
will simultaneously carry us further afield while safeguard-
ing against important misunderstandings likely to vitiate
the entire enquiry. Firstly, Cragg concedes that the historical Islam of the Prophet is a decisive and genuine 'religious'
achievement: it is a faith that helped Muhammad to
achieve his own destiny as a religious reformer and offered
spiritual pabulum to those who have espoused the Islamic
creed in subsequent centuries. Yet this Islamic story, contends Cragg, by the very fact of its marked worldly success,
drives the Christian conscience to wonder whether or not
it is *religiously* authentic. How is it that religious truth
has here the benefit of being the hero, so to speak, of a
spectacular success story? Can it be that the triumph of
Islam has been gained at too heavy a cost, the cost of
compromising the prophetic office? Surely, given that we
live in a world addicted to sin and rejection, as the Koran
itself testifies, the phenomenally rapid and enduring success of Islam stands in need of explanation.

Cragg identifies this as a significant worry. Precisely
because Islam has a largely authentic 'religious' dimension,
he contends, it is worthwhile for the Christian (and indeed
the believing Muslim) to try to assess the problematic
nature of the 'political' elements which, by Christian criteria painfully hammered out in the ethos of Gethsemane,
look like betrayals of genuine spirituality. In other words,
if Islam were a partly or entirely false faith, there would
be no moral problem about its 'political' involvement or

worldly achievement. It is only because Islam does indeed qualify as a genuine faith that one needs to be perturbed by its power dimension. Religiously as well as morally, these are fair reservations, surely; and Christians and Muslims alike have the right to their own consciences.

Secondly, Cragg is not opposed to militancy *per se*. There is nothing wrong with the *right* kind of enthusiasm, the proper brand of zeal. But what are the resources of a truly faithful militancy? Cragg's response is as simple as it is uncompromising: the prophet has no truck with worldly power. What fellowship hath faith with force? The prophet's only armour is the word preached. His defencelessness and vulnerability in the face of the world's anger is precisely a part of his witness. It is not extraneous to his vocation; rather it constitutes it. The weapons of his struggle are purely verbal. In Cragg's view, what is religiously suspect about Islam is its characteristic tendency to join together the demands of the divine imperative – shared by all the theisms – with militancy understood in terms of physical capacity and power. But, concludes Cragg, borrowing Shakespeare's implied verdict from *Henry V* (Act IV, scene 1, lines 149, 151), blood is no argument – least of all, one might add, in matters of the spirit. A thoughtful reservation, let us grant; everyone alike has the right to conscience in matters of moment.

These are preliminary considerations. The thoughts here have lengthy careers both intrinsically and in their entailments. The two chapters that follow will explore the territory. The New Testament stance on the place of worldly power in the coming messianic kingdom provides an apt starting-point; and it is to this that I must now turn.

3   The Third Temptation

1

There is no passage parallel to Matthew 4:1–11 in the Koran. But let us suppose, for the sake of a theological experiment, that the Devil, no stranger to the Koranic world, comes to Muhammad and offers him all the kingdoms of the world on condition that he worship him. Would Muhammad's retort have been any different from that of Jesus or indeed any other messenger of God? No; in fact, Jesus' own response is thoroughly Islamic. So what's our quarrel?

The quarrel, as Cragg sees it, is that Muhammad, unlike Jesus, accepted power as a means of achieving religious ends. But power, Cragg counsels, is no part of the arsenal. Though God is of course all-powerful in the Christian vision, it is his love that seeks to achieve triumphs over the recalcitrant human heart.

The third temptation experienced by Jesus in the desert (Matthew 4:8–9; Mark 1:12–13; Luke 4:2–17) is in effect a temptation to interpret the messianic chore as essentially political, as power-centred. Offered the cup of power, Jesus refuses it on *religious* grounds. Divine ends require divine means; and power is not one of them. Human perversity requires a suffering Messiah – not, as contemporary Judaic wisdom required, an armed and 'victorious' one. In the event, Christ is said to have chosen the cup of suffering love in one of the supreme tragedies of religious history.

I will need at this stage to request both Muslim and Christian readers to exercise care and caution. The Muslim will, no doubt, be offended by the implied suggestion that Muhammad 'chickened out' in the hour of crisis; Christians are likely to entertain triumphalist sentiments about Christ standing his ground where others of a similar vocation retreated. There are at stake here complex worries about the essence of Islam, the essence of the Christian outlook, and, in turn, a tangle of issues about the ministry of Jesus in an Islamic-koranic (as opposed to New Testament Christian) perspective. I will proceed step by step and pause for reflection at a number of points.

2

Cragg writes, with evident approval, of those servants of God's word – men like Jeremiah, pre-eminently – who prefer a worthy failure of their ministry to an unworthy success (*Muhammad and the Christian*, pp. 43ff). Within the potentially polemical context of the debate, the implication about the moral unworthiness of Muhammad's success is unmistakable. Cragg himself goes on to make this explicit. Was then Muhammad's political career compromised by his involvement with power? Does worldly success always tell against the moral (or religious) worth of a truly prophetic ministry? Is political failure the only guarantee of authenticity of mission?

Before we begin to answer these questions directly, it is wise to strengthen Cragg's case. The Koran, argues Cragg, is completely silent on the 'failed' servants (except for Jesus, whose ministry is radically reinterpreted). This silence is taken by Cragg to be a very eloquent comment on the ultimate character of a koranic religiosity that is, arguably, internally coherent yet blind to alternative patterns of divine grace. To include prophets such as Jeremiah in the scriptural corpus would, conjectures Cragg, 'have been to entertain an intolerable interrogation of Muslim assumption and assurance' (*Muhammad and the Christian*, p. 43). It is true of course that Jesus' career is discussed in relative detail in the Muslim Scriptures, though his ministry 'ended' in apparent failure. But, as Cragg notices, this ministry is radically reinterpreted – and, for Christians, radically attenuated if not distorted – in the Koran in order to align it with Muslim norms of genuine religion. Jesus was denied political success while receiving purely 'religious' honours; Muhammad had the best of both worlds. In an unusual manoeuvre, the Koran adopts a spectacular rescue mission for the obedient Jesus, thus frustrating the Jewish will to impiety and vindicating the 'politically failed' servant. Failure is not allowed the last word; tragedy finds no foothold in the Islamic mind.

Let us examine Cragg's contention that no mention of the failed messengers is to be found in the Muslim scriptures. Is this true? The Koran's choice of messengers whose careers are to be rehearsed is representative rather than comprehensive. It is possible therefore that some prophets not mentioned by name in the scriptures were failures by worldly criteria but are none the less recognized as having been true to their office. Certainly, there are messengers without pronounced political ambitions – Job, Zachariah, John, Joseph, Jacob and others – who receive extensive mention in the sacred volume. And the Koran, like all sacred literature, rejects the identification of success by profane standards.

Even so, Cragg's point remains. What of Jeremiah? And why does Job's passionately accusatory address to his Lord receive no mention at all? The koranic outlook is, I would argue, fully compatible with the view that some faithful spokesmen were political failures. They delivered their trust from God, stood their ground, died or were in some cases martyred by the sinful establishment, and consequently did not live to see the fruits, political or otherwise, of their endeavours. Such men's spirituality is as perfect in its way as is the spirituality of those – like Muhammad, Moses and Solomon – whose careers resulted in political success. If political achievement is not a proof of religious authenticity, political failure is not a necessary condition of it either.

If God had willed, Jesus could have been martyred rather than translated: he could have failed in a straightforward way and done so within Islamic presuppositions. Equally, as Chapter 13 Verse 40 of the Koran hints,

Muhammad could have died in Mecca without living to
see Islam established with the sanction of power in Medina.
These possibilities are not theologically vetoed by any doctrine of the Koran.

There is a view, held by some modern Muslims, that
Jesus' spirituality remained immature on account of its
failure to blossom into worldly political success. This view
is both un-Islamic and demonstrably unworthy of genuine
religion. The koranic view is that God ordains a particular
ministry for a particular messenger, tailored to time and
place. The essence of his vocation is always *islam*, i.e.,
complete and unqualified submission to the will and dictates of the Almighty. The details differ. Some prophets
have been more successful – in a worldly sense – than
others. For some, their mission remained incomplete: they
failed to get their community to repent in time. For others,
the ending was drastic: the impious society rose up in
arms and exterminated the warner and his group. But each
messenger has his religious authenticity in his mission. It
is true that God has, according to the Koran, exalted some
prophets above others. But the ranking is, wisely, not
given; and it is not implied that political success is one of
the criteria for assessing religious worth. That some Muslims have, in a triumphalist spirit, thought otherwise should
not seriously interest us here.

It is true of course that God has granted a spectacular
victory to the Arabian messenger. And God does whatever
He pleases on account of His power and wisdom, being
bound neither by the whims of rejectors nor the prejudices
of believers.

When Cragg claims that the Koran's reluctance to dis-
cuss the ministry of men such as Jeremiah is due to a
diffidence about its own preferred religious norms, it is
difficult to avoid the suspicion of some partisan Christian
sensibility at work. (Cragg is a missionary to Islam if not
to Muslims: he wants to Christianize that faith if not convert its adherents. 'Subvert if not convert' is an apt slogan
here.) In any case, only a reading thoroughly imbued with
Christian preconceptions could succeed in detecting any

such lack of confidence. When I read the same text – and here I can speak on behalf of many Muslims – I see that the Koran expresses, decrees rather, its own normative views with sustained clarity and irresistible force of conviction as well as language. That many passages about prophetic failure are dark and anxious is beyond dispute. Yet anxiety of that kind is not evidence of diffidence about the truth of the vision on whose behalf it is felt. It is evidence rather of a desire to see the appropriate ideals fulfilled in a recalcitrant world.

It is fair to conclude that there is no theological reason for the view that a messenger's commitment to *islam* is incomplete unless it bears fruit in political success. To be sure, many Muslims have seen politically unsuccessful prophetic careers as amounting merely to conventional speech-making. The real issue at stake here between Muslims and Christians is whether or not worldly success can legitimately crown religious achievement. And the Koran does presuppose that religion is not allergic to worldly triumph.

3

In *Jesus and the Muslim*, in a series of heart-searching meditations (especially on pp. 126–7), Cragg raises what he aptly calls the problem of the kind of victory pertinent and proper to religious truth. I have just argued that Islam does not, in principle, preclude from the ambit of God's varied grace the kind of victory exemplified in the ministry of Jesus *as understood by Christians*. Many Muslims have indeed dismissed such a possibility as unworthy of true religion. The Koran's own reservations are purely historical, not doctrinal. Christ did not suffer in the manner claimed by Christians; he didn't have to, though he was certainly ready to do so. If Jesus had been seen as succesfully crucified, the Koran would still have refused to draw any potentially tragic conclusion. Crucifixion or no crucifixion, Jesus was victorious. For he had, in both cases, submitted himself to the will and ordinance of God. He was *muslim* – resigned to the will of his Lord. And that is sufficient.

Christians need to listen to the Islamic story here carefully. The beginnings of Islam do indeed constitute a success story. But that success is only genuine because it is the kind of success pertinent to faith. If it were improper – if it were patronized by some diabolic sovereignty – it would no longer be a success in the eyes of the highest arbiter of value. This is the Muslim conviction.

What, then, is the kind of victory appropriate to faith? In one sense, the answer, surprisingly, is 'None'. For God's views do not stand in need of the patronage of victory in the human world. The divine truth contains its own guarantee of success and worth. The word of God cannot fail in its truth, in its claim to metaphysically secure status; at most it can fail in its acceptance by us – fallible, sinful men and women. And so much the worse for us. This is the sense in which the word of God necessarily has the last word. Whatever we may think, scripture is the ultimate truth. In that sense, God is certainly independent of our response to His holy summons – whether in penitent submission or impenitent rejection.

Cragg's concern is, of course, a different one, though he himself never makes the necessary distinctions here. What is success in matters of the spirit? How should the word of God 'succeed' in our human, all too human and wayward world? How should the messenger ensure the success and victory of God's cause? Granted that God's causes are always victorious in the last analysis, how should a prophet crown them with success in the mundane context of impiety and opposition? Granted that God always wins eventually the war if not all the battles, what are the weapons His spokesmen should use?

One might say that Jesus responded very differently to the crisis of Israel's *kufr* (disbelief) than Muhammad did to the crisis of Qurashi rejection and scorn. Christ interpreted *kufr* to be a malady deep within the human soul – a malady only love could cure, a love that assumed a 'passively' suffering vocation. Muhammad, one might

argue, interpreted the experience of rejection as necessitat-
ing social and political struggle in alliance with the perennial concern with the mischief of the sinful heart. The
alternatives as posed by Christians are false both in fact and
in implication. For Muhammad was concerned to eradicate
hypocrisy precisely because of his concern with the inner
self; and Christ's supposed repudiation of the political
sector has none the less retained significances that are
manifestly political. Of course, neither reformer could
have doubted the power of God's love and mercy. The
question remains whether or not a victory attained through
patience, prayer *and* political strife and struggle is worthy
of the name in matters of the spirit. Cragg insists that the
only truly godly resources are preaching in alliance with
patience and prayer. God, despite His former militancy as
recorded in the Old Testament, has recently washed His
hands of the whole dirty political side of the affair. The
debate must continue.

4

The quarrel between Muslims and Christians is over what
Cragg describes as 'the politicization of religion' (*Muhammad and the Christian*, pp. 48, 66) whereby the divine
arsenal is supplemented by political power. Now this problematic phrase already arguably implies a perspective alien
to Islam. It leads Cragg to make a number of uncharacteristically hasty and, in my view, radically untrue judgements
concerning the essence of the Muslim faith. Cragg is convinced, for reasons connected with his Christian outlook,
that it was the deep-rooted pagan opposition to Muhammad's Meccan ministry that necessarily 'politicized' the
initial and purely religious faith of Islam. *Prima facie* at
least, this view seems to beg the question. It begs a crucial
question against the standard Muslim understanding of
the nature of Islam. Islam was, in its very essence and
conception, a faith incorporating the political dimension
as integral to its own self-image. Is it possible to 'politicize'
such a religion? It is not as though Islam acquires political

temper for the first time in the antagonistic circumstance of Medina.

Any view of the political which characterizes it as a feature extraneous to the religious ideal is totally foreign to the Koran. Islam was incomplete in the Meccan context; it found completion in the Medinan state. When Cragg argues that Islam was politicized he means that involvement with the political sector – the attempt to conquer the entire pagan power structure – was an accretion, if a legitimate one, to an originally 'pure' religious faith. But this assumption is false. For one can only politicize a faith that is originally apolitical in the sense required by Cragg. And in that sense one can quite meaningfully speak of the politicization of Buddhism or Christianity. When the religion in question is Islam, there is a temptation – to which Christian critics readily succumb – to transport, indeed smuggle in, alien conceptions of the 'religious' and the 'political' wing. At no stage in its development does the Islamic outlook record any recognition of any territory of human concern that is outside the range of the religious imperative. It is the critic who first separates the political sector – understood in the narrow sense popular with Western writers – and then makes its alignment with the religious wing – understood in an equally restricted sense – into a matter for moral reproach. To be sure, all faiths, including Christianity, necessarily have dealings with the political establishments of their day. That is uncontroversial. But Islam, by its very nature, seeks to absorb political community in the larger desire to sanctify it. Muslims do not, in other words, see the political life and political institutions as outside of, or extrinsic to, the demands and regulations of faith.

Cragg's understanding of Islam as essentially – that is, originally – a purely religious world view that got caught up later, for good reasons, in political conflict, is radically mistaken. And the fortunate thing – for us – is that Cragg fully reveals his misunderstanding. He does this in a long and crucial passage in *Muhammad and the Christian*. Cragg is here asserting that while faiths may well need to compromise with force as they become traditions, they should not do so in their very origins. Consequently, he finds it odd that Islam unashamedly incorporates the power dimension into its original setting. Since the point is complex and controversial, it is best to quote directly:

Faiths may well discern this compromising necessity in their entail. Is it well that it should be hallowed in their origin? [. . .] To the Christian mind, nurtured by Jesus and the Gospels, it will always be a burden and a tragedy that force has been so uncomplicatedly enshrined in the very canons of Islam via the patterns of the *Sirah*. For that sufficient reason, any appreciation of Muhammad *in situ* must resolutely retain the contrasted meaning of the love that suffers as the Christ. Christianity in history has so far and so readily besmirched its own originating nature as to make that resolve paramount in all its external relationships, lest its own temptation should be mistaken by others for its – or their – proper norms. (p. 51).

This is an extremely important passage in *Muhammad and the Christian*. Now, when Cragg writes that he can well sympathize with the tendency of men to debase their own ideals, no one will quarrel with him. That is a well-documented fact – an observation of the failings of our common humanity. Christians and, to a far lesser extent, Muslims, have much to be ashamed of in their respective histories. But failure to live up to one's own ideal is one thing; failure to live up to someone else's ideal is quite another. The model behind Cragg's critique is, unsurprisingly, Christian in impulse. And, at least from a modern Protestant standpoint, he is absolutely right in saying that Christians have compromised themselves in having recourse to secular power. Such a move may well be a categorical departure from the norms implicit in any authentic *imitatio Christi*. But Cragg is begging the question against Muhammad and his followers when he claims that *their* use of force was equally compromising. For, surely, the Islamic ideal recognizes the legitimacy of force. Thus, a Christian compromises his moral integrity in having *any* recourse to coercive methods to effect reform. But a Muslim only compromises himself – if we use standards intrinsic to Islam – by *mis-*

using force. For Islam does not see power in itself as necessarily destructive. Indeed, power is no more inherently corrupting than sexuality or knowledge, or the appetite for food. Men err when they lapse from the appropriate ideal governing the proper recruitment and enjoyment of a particular facility. And this error is discerned by reference to a religious ideal that is ordained for the tuition and guidance of a fallible humanity.

Cragg is perturbed by the fact that Islam incorporates power into its basic canons. But, disturbing or not, surely what this decision to incorporate the political wing really shows is that the involvement with power is integral – a part of the definition of Islam – and not, as Cragg would have us believe, an act of compromise necessitated by later recalcitrant circumstance. One can now readily see why the phrase 'politicization of Islam' is, strictly speaking, senseless. For it implies an originally apolitical faith. And Islam was never apolitical; it was a faith that was always insisting on its involvement with worldly power. Like the ministries of David and Solomon, Muhammad's own ministry was a thoroughly political affair wherever it could be, both in Mecca and in Medina. To see his vocation as acquiring a political colouring after the *Hijra* – to see the *Hijra* as a 'temptation' – is to misunderstand Islam.

We can well understand why Christians wish to see power as a temptation. For that is precisely what it is – for the contemporary Christian conscience. A radical and inclusive reservation about power is now a part of the Christian ideal. To be sure, the quoted passage from Matthew is not a repudiation of power but rather of idolatry. But even so, early Pauline Christianity was indeed distinguished by its refusal to seek the protection of political sanction. Christians saw power as a temptation. Notwithstanding severe persecution under Roman rule and less severe persecution by the Jewish establishment, Christians remained loyal to the image of a suffering Christ. Widespread martyrdom among early Christian communities is an undeniable fact of ancient history. However, in subsequent centuries, Christians did indeed compromise –

sometimes eagerly – with the powerful forces of the world, wielding the sword in practice while periodically decrying its use in their abstract theology. The Muslim must, for religious reasons, look with compassion and forgiveness upon those who fail to live up to what are often seen as impossibly high ideals. (To a Muslim, they are not high ideals at all, but simply an irresponsible refusal to address the pressing injustices of the real world.) But there can be no doubt that the Christian faithful have been, from a modern theological viewpoint, guilty of a betrayal of principle.

Cragg, then, is misled by the problematic phrase 'the politicization of religion'. Such a phrase significantly skews the debate. The expression may be properly used only if some reservations about its use in discussions of Islam are formulated and published from the start. Otherwise one begs the question against a faith that recognizes no distinction between the religious and the political. To say that Islam was politicized on account of its early hostile encounter with the Qurashī establishment is to introduce an acceptably Christian squint.

To see clearly why the phrase 'the politicizing of religion' is unacceptable, it is well to compare it with the less sinister-sounding expression 'the religionizing of the political'. Both phrases are, of course, from the standpoint of Islam, strictly speaking incorrect as a description of the Muslim involvement with the political life. But the latter expression is to be preferred, for it describes a process much closer to what the Islamic ideal actually entails. The political life is brought within the purview of divine demand and dictate. One might say that the political has been sanctified and purified once it has been brought under the aegis of revealed faith.

5

In *Muhammad and the Christian*, Cragg often writes as though Muhammad's troubles were over after the *Hijra*. In Mecca, then, this powerless but conscientious man had voiced a bitter jeremiad against the rich and powerful who occupied positions of undeserved privilege. The wealthy and proud Quraysh ignored the just plea of the powerless man. And then, after due consideration, the prophet realized that power was the cure for all the ills around him – including the scorn and haughtiness of the pagan Arabs. After thirteen years of earnest quest, pacific labour and religious anxiety, Muhammad had found the much-sought 'short-cuts to ease the calling' (*Muhammad and the Christian*, p. 44).

It is utterly naive, when one considers the historical details, to discern any easing of the prophetic vocation in the post-*Hijra* years. Many Medinan passages in the Koran warn of greater 'trials' (*fitan*) – in the extremely rich sense of the original Arabic – yet to come. Thus for example, *Sūra* 8, vv. 65–6, cautions the infant community that though it has one victory to its account – the decisive Battle of Badr – there are yet greater tests forthcoming which will thoroughly 'try' the mettle of the believers.

The concern with ceaseless *jihād* (struggle) is central to the Koran. And a commitment to *jihād* is precisely a way of making sure there are no 'short-cuts to ease the calling'. The Koran and its prophetic recipient are both concerned to condemn sinful complacency, any notion that the end is in sight. Muhammad remained in the field – fighting, praying, repenting, witnessing to the glory of God – until his dying day. There is a marked stress on the importance of self-purification and 'struggle in the way of God' (*al-jihād fi sabīli'Llāh*) in the Medinan *Sūras*.

It was in fact at Medina that the Prophet began training the *ahl al-ṣuffa* (the 'People of the Veranda') – those ascetic and saintly men who became the ideal for later Islamic spirituality. It was in Medina, too, that the annual fast of Ramadan, one of the most world-denying Islamic rites, was institutionalized and observed. Any reading, no matter how concerned to attenuate the rich import of the Medinan passages, must still discern a rigour of moral demand that is hard to supersede. All the believers, particularly the Prophet himself, knew they had miles to go before they slept. To find here any easing, any attenuation of demand, any drop in the moral temperature, requires bias on the part of the reader.

We must pursue this point a little. The Prophet himself saw militant struggle as a necessary evil; he did not enjoy it. But, as he knew, if the commitment to Islam requires violent struggle against injustice, then so be it. To concede that God is great (*Allāhu akbar*) and yet to prefer one's own opinions is not to make for sincerity of conviction. For Muhammad, the *abdication* of political struggle would have been the real compromise, the real short-cut to ease the vocation. As with most arguments of polemical import, Cragg's contention can easily be turned on its head: to refuse to accept violent struggle when circumstances are thought to demand it is as compromising a gesture as accepting it when it is thought morally preferable to eschew it. The question of compromise is not resolved *a priori* but rather in relationship to an agent's perception of moral worth and lapse. And seen in this light – the only correct perspective here, incidentally – we can see why Jesus and Muhammad could have entertained opposed notions whose authenticity is relative to social context. If Christ really rejected the political option, that is no ground for every prophet to reject the political option. He was presumably right to do so, given the circumstances of his mission; nothing follows about the normative deportment of messengers fatefully placed in different circumstances. This is one of the many instances in which some idiosyncratic yet proper feature of Jesus' ministry (in Christian-New Testament perspective) is mistakenly seen as supplying a central criterion for assessing the authenticity of the prophetic mission in general.

Muhammad was a conscientious man. Indeed, it is impossible to study his life objectively without being impressed by the sheer severity of his iconoclastic conscience. The Koran itself – Muhammad's guide in all circumstances – lays the axe at the root of every facility, whim or desire, that could conceivably serve to attenuate, sell short or compromise the service of God. It is important to note in this context that Muhammad and his group were, at the outset, reluctant to use force even in defence. The Koran itself, in the chapter entitled *The Pilgrimage*, sanctions violent struggle in the case of those against whom war is made, who are unjustly expelled from their habitations solely on account of their saying 'Our Lord is God'. Fighting was hateful to the believers; yet it was necessary. God, counsels the sacred volume, may put much good in a thing we perceive to be unpleasant (Koran 2:216). Our ultimate allegiance is to God; and if the use of force is required for the preservation of justice and witness, we must be willing to use it.

Now, if the Koran had seen the use of force as a form of compromise – as Cragg implies – it would certainly have condemned it. For it is precisely the repudiation of any and every form of compromise that constitutes the iconoclastic conscience. The Prophet is instructed to reject the pagans' formula for reconciliation through religious compromise: 'to you your religion, to me my religion'. That extremely uncooperative sentiment eventually led to much bloodshed and unhappiness and total débâcle. Again, the Koran's many uncompromising verses that place the bond of faith above that of blood, marriage and tribe, led to much domestic friction, pitching brother against brother, severing families and tribes, while the slackening of alliances with the pagans caused considerable commercial losses for the Muslims and, in its wake, extreme poverty. But that is Islam. It is not a religion of comfort – of comfortable accommodations with rejection and sin. To say *Allāhu akbar* and yet to prefer one's own whims is to invite the charge of hypocrisy. To refuse to engage in violent struggle when one recognizes the need for it is effectively to compromise with evil, to sell short the service of God, to deny the greatness of God – and to allow the over-refinements of intelligent hypocrisy to vindicate the resulting lapse from the ideal.

Nor is this to deny the possibility of abusing the facility of power. The success that power brings must itself be worthy of religious acceptance. God does not patronize victories that betray His sacred purposes to profane ends. In the hour of triumph, the hundred and tenth chapter of the Koran instructs the Prophet to 'sanctify' his success lest it should become one patronized by some profane, inwardly idolatrous though outwardly Islamic, sovereignty. Muhammad knew he had miles to go before he slept.

6

In *Jesus and the Muslim*, Cragg attempts to indicate a central discrepancy in koranic thought about the issue of collective evil confronting individualistic patterns of piety. Unwittingly, he here provides a justification for the post-*Hijra* ministry of Muhammad. The context of the debate is a much-quoted koranic remark: 'No soul, already laden, bears the burden of another' (Koran 6:164; 17:15). Cragg is trying to express, in a manner congenial to Muslim instincts, the Pauline concern with the status of original (or Adamic) sin (*Jesus and the Muslim*, pp. 216–25).

Cragg – straying rather far from orthodoxy – explains that original sin is not properly to be interpreted as an individual act, committed by Adam, and transmitted in some kind of travesty of justice to all subsequent men and women. The issue is not the historical one of inheritance but rather the perennial one of perversity. We are all human; and Adam is the typical mortal.

So far, so good. Adam is the symbol of mankind, a symbol of collective pride and sinfulness. Cragg claims that 'this human solidarity makes for dimensions of human evil which a purely individual view of relationships is likely to overlook' (*op. cit.* p. 219). He argues that the koranic view of evil is, in general, 'very personalistic' – laying emphasis on the private individual, his individual choices, his individual vindication or condemnation. Yet, continues Cragg, this is to overlook 'the evil of structures, of states and society, of collectives and institutions . . .' (*ibid.*). And where 'motives of personal selfishness become corporate, or find excuse in the expediency to which things political and economic readily appeal, then the collective selfishness intensifies the wrong' (*ibid*.). In this context, Cragg writes with approval of the obscure Egyptian writer Muḥammad Kāmil Ḥusayn's 'scepticism about the amenability of public "causes" to the moral restraints and standards that might weigh with private people' (*ibid*.; Kāmil Ḥusayn, *The City of Evil*).

Yet surely one should, if one is fair, immediately note the implications of this train of thought for our earlier assessment of Muhammad's ministry. If it is true that collectives and groups develop their own momentum of evil, as Cragg implies, that the consequences of even undeniably private actions are far from private, it may well be the case that the right way of 'dealing' with collective evil must itself be alert to the structural-public dimension of human wrongdoing. Yet precisely this recognition is denied, for reasons adduced *a priori*, by Christian critics of Islam. For any such recognition serves conclusively to justify Muhammad's decision to alter not merely recalcitrant individual consciences but rather also to come to terms with the entire power-structure that had resisted his preachings. To be sure, such a reckoning must itself respect the constraints of religious principle and right conduct. The political programme must engage men and women who are long-suffering, working with and within individual consciences, never upon, let alone against, the promptings of the individual conscientious office.

The point is elemental. The Christian thinker cannot have it both ways. If there are social dimensions to individual evil, then a right form of piety, in its confrontation with the evil of structures, must have the resources to deal with the social, not merely the personal, consequences of such evil. And this is particularly true given the fact that collective evil is very likely in practice to assume militant forms. To concede, as Christians do, that evil takes on a structural aspect, yet to deny the need for a corresponding form of reckoning that is alert precisely to this structural dimension is, in effect, to make for an unrealistic and immature model of piety.

Cragg's other points about the koranic dictum concerning the soul's individual responsibility are well taken. The burden of the soul is that of the guilty – or better shame-stricken – conscience introspectively aware of its own wrongdoings. That is the intended meaning here. Of course, there are others around us who impose various burdens of pain and suffering – burdens that are strictly not our own in their origin but certainly ours in the bearing. As friends, enemies, lovers, mothers, brothers, fathers, citizens, we contribute to one another's pains. In that sense, virtually every burdened soul bears the burden of another. But the divine reckoning that awaits the individual cannot be transferred.

7

One might say that the Koran, like the Bhagavad Gita, was revealed on a battlefield. The forces of good and evil are entrenched in their positions. The Koran's Arabian context is one of militant impiety versus militant righteousness; the profane establishment was thoroughly opposed to the sacred cause. Unsurprisingly, as Cragg reminds us, the actual context of the Scripture's incidence is significantly reflected in its tone, its method and mood.

Fair enough; but then come the somewhat wistful musings of a Cragg 'wishing he might savour the message of divine transcendence in a constituency more congenial to its wonder, less stubborn in its waywardness, than the one Muhammad had to face in Mecca, so that his quality might be known in a joyful availing of his word' (*Muhammad and the Christian*, pp. 22–3). An idle wish, of course, even at best; and a thoroughly misguided one at worst. For there is only one constituency proper to the word of God – the human constituency. And that constituency is typically not 'congenial' in the required way. Unfortunate, to be sure; but there we have it. It was not congenial in the days of Moses; it was not congenial in the days of Muhammad. And it has not become so in the contemporary world. Impiety has, does, and will always assume militant forms in its opposition to righteousness. That is the way of the world – and one very conclusively demon-strated, ironically, in the ministry of Jesus. The world of first-century Palestine did not, to put it no more strongly, provide a congenial constituency; it was not lacking in perversity or the over-confidence of evil, both perennial features of the human condition.

God works out His purposes in the real world, not through our daydreams. His constituency is our human, all too human, world. To attenuate the obstinacy of man, to reduce the actual dimensions of human perversity, whether for purposes practical or abstract, is effectively to wish for a constituency that has little in common with our own world. It is, in effect, to ask for illusions. Reality, both natural and political, has no great desire to reflect the wishes and slogans of the pious will.

These observations relate importantly to issues of political violence, as will be seen more clearly in the following chapters. This harsh and indifferent world may not be the only one worth describing – fantasy has its rewards – but it is necessarily the only one worth changing. That is why any realistic scripture must deal with human beings as they actually are, not as we would ideally like them to be. There is no constituency more worthy of wonder than the real world.

4   Giving God His Due

1

'All a poet can do today is warn. That is why the true
poets must be truthful.' So wrote Wilfred Owen, killed in
1918, in a draft preface to a collection of poems he was
intending to publish (*Pelican Guide to English Literature*,
pp. 166–7). Why the note of inadequacy and despair? *All*
a poet can do today is warn. Isn't that enough? Warning
is a difficult and lengthy profession; it is indeed the role of
the prophet. Within the Koran, Muhammad is frequently
referred to as a warner, his mission centred on counselling
the pagan conscience about the calamitous consequences
of rejection. Both the prophetic warning and the reckoning
it embodied were, as it happens, destined to assume dramatic, including violent, forms as the profane establishment confronted the Islamic cause on both sides of the
Hijra divide.

The note of despair is justified; warning does not always
avail. To be sure, one may preach on behalf of the good
and just cause. Yet the world rarely casts its vote for truth.
Unfortunate, to be sure; but that's altogether the evident
reality of the human constituency. There are indeed recognizable moral superiorities that attach to the words and
petitions of good men, and, moreover, these superiorities
are rarely seen as being negligible by the contemporaneous
audience – and almost never seen in that light by posterity.
(As Nietzsche has it, history is merely the record of 'bad'
men who were *later* 'baptized' good men.) So the good
man's words and his cause are alike praiseworthy and seen
as such often enough. But perversity reduces his contemporaneous audience, for few listen to him.

Nor is this due mainly to heedlessness, or *ghafla*, one of the Koran's richest and most frequent terms. Heedlessness hardly takes the full measure of the sheer depth and variety of opposition to the good. It is a depth clearly well beyond *ghafla* in the nature of its roots, in the quality of its motivation, in the tenacity of its intention. For, certainly, men's opposition to the prophetic – or the good, if you like – cannot properly be reduced to the level of the casual or even regular and deliberate neglect of religious norms. It is certainly not mere indifference to truth or justice. Rather, the opposition is close to a conspiratorial and sinister hatred of the good, an intelligent animus towards what is just and equitable. The conflict here is inveterate: the Qurashi establishment was deeply determined to dislodge 'Allah and His messenger'. Wilful and cynical verbal rejection give way in due course to armed defiance and brutal violence against righteousness – all familiar features of the prophetic *sīra* (biography) as it unfolds on both sides of the *Hijra* divide, providing as it does an instructively depressing commentary on the profane capacity for militant evil and perversity.

2

'All a prophet should do is warn.' Cragg might well have penned these very words – for the whole logic of his position inexorably implies some such verdict. Like the poet, the prophet and the preacher must also rely on purely verbal weapons. The pen had better be mightier than the sword. Hearts are to be won; and all the peaceful instruments of prophecy – namely, persuasion, tact, endurance, patience, persistence – are of limited assistance in a world whose enmity to truth is neither casual nor intermittent.

Yet there is no alternative. There are, Cragg tells us, no short-cuts here; a hasty kind of militancy would compromise the quality of one's allegiance to the good and the just. There is no way of easing the anguish. One warns; people ignore it; one prays and suffers patiently. And again; and again. That's the way of the man of God; that's the prophetic vocation. After all, 'What fellowship hath faith with force?'

Fair enough; but evil can assume more militant forms, develop a greater reach in its operations. What is one to do in the face of threats to the warner's life and property? Cragg's answer is predictable: helplessness is one of the liabilities of the prophetic office. It is part of one's calling. To feel constantly vulnerable in the face of the cruel powers of the world – of *dunyā* in koranic vocabulary – is the true hallmark of the man of God.

Might we not reverently question such a verdict? Granted that the wrong kind of militancy may merely inspire – and then conspire with – more sophisticated forms of the very evil one seeks to eradicate, must one remain utterly helpless in the face of wrongdoing, unable to intervene forcefully even to protect the rights of others? Granted that overwhelming suffering is often part and parcel of any genuine attachment to truth in this corrupt world, is the attempt to alleviate distress through armed defence necessarily an act of compromise? Must suffering in sheer defencelessness be the *only* hallmark of the truly prophetic career? Is the *only* right attitude, then, to plunge defenceless into the thick of battle only to be duly martyred by the ruthless forces of a world that constantly harbours the impulse to an impiety unqualified by the mitigations of conscience or retrospective mercy?

3

'It takes fifty years', wrote W. B. Yeats in a letter dated April 1936, 'for a poet's weapons to influence the issue' (*The Letters of W. B. Yeats*, ed. Allan Wade, p. 851). Why fifty? Why not a more generous and less arbitrary estimate – of an age, a century, even a millennium? Yeats here provides us with an apt perspective on the unarmed literary warrior's felt need for patience in a world addicted to the logic of coercion and hasty militancy. In his own context, the Irish poet is referring to his poem 'The Second Coming', written in 1920 as a protest against the military cult of force and violence. The pen is Yeats' only weapon; and it need not achieve the 'influence' the poet seeks. Certainly, one needs all the patience one can muster.

Suppose, however, that a poet's or preacher's 'weapons' failed to influence the issue – even in fifty years or a century. For men are at liberty to ignore the plea of the just messenger, and they can turn a deaf ear indefinitely. (In 1940, W. H. Auden rejected his political poetry of the 1930s on the grounds that 'poetry makes nothing happen'.) If so, patience is not the issue any longer. The problem is to see truth triumphant in a world attached to illusory and false ideals. And such an ambition cannot always be realized without the recruitment of force.

Where goodness has knocked for admission long and in vain, it is surely the better part of wisdom to force entry. Once in the house, once goodness has made her case, it should be possible for the miscreants to reject her case with impunity.

Nor is this purely Islamic – partisan – reasoning. This reasoning is in fact *precisely* identical to the Christian reasoning in defence of Christianity's recruitment of power after the early centuries of persecution and powerlessness. It has been said against those who, like Cragg, obstinately and no doubt unreasonably insist on commending a Christianity devoid of the benefits of power, that they themselves would not be in a position to be believers in such a 'powerless' creed if power had not, at some important hour, secured its future and brought it to prominence on the historical stage.

4

If men are to do good effectively, they must act in association; and it is not to be supposed that any form of association, no matter how large, can afford to rest upon nothing more than community of purpose, implicit agreement of opinion or even the cementing influence of charismatic leadership. If such associations, along with the intensely shared vision they embody, are to stand up against external attack by a hostile world or even against the menace of internal dissension, these must be able to count daily not only upon the firm loyalty of members but also upon the widespread recognition of the need for struggle – including, unfortunately, violent struggle – against those profane forces inclined to be intolerant of the good. This, it is clear, is the reasoning of the Koran in that matter of armed struggle (*jihād*) which has so long alienated many Western readers of the text.

'What of individual meekness and pacific protest?' So asks the Christian conscience in good faith. Cragg implies that Muhammad did not encourage allegiance to the ideals of meekness and non-violent resistance because these would have, in any case, inspired little enthusiasm among the seventh-century pagan Arabs (*Muhammad and the Christian*, p. 40). Yet the ideals of Islam, avowedly at variance with pacific philosophies, did not inspire much enthusiasm either. Hence the painful history of early Islam in the Hijaz – the Western Arabian peninsula. In fact, the desire to see ideals fulfilled is not properly a function of their viability alone; it also depends in part on their perceived moral importance and validity. As for the ideals of pacifism and quiet protest, it is worth asking whether these have had much purchase in *any* society, including any 'Christian' society. One might see this very lack of popularity to be a sign of their supposed nobility; yet it is wise to resist the conclusion that impracticability and unrealism are the true hallmarks of the religious ideal.

5

A Muhammad face to face with a Pilate would have given the Roman chap a lot more to do than merely wash his hands. But precisely that, argues Cragg, is the whole problem with 'political religion'. The prophet should stick to his guns, in a manner of speaking of course, and these are patience and prayer.

Islam, continues Cragg, is founded on one major error concerning the achievements of militancy in the religious life. Unfortunately, for the Muslim militants, faith in a fighting posture compromises itself by any forceful engagement with the forces that seek to oppose it. The recruitment of power, pontificates Cragg, must necessarily forfeit 'the very quality of truth and mercy which justified it in the first place' (*Muhammad and the Christian*, p. 32). This is one of the many self-defeating consequences of faith when it makes allegiance with worldly power. Small wonder, then, that Christ saw it as a temptation to be resisted. To establish by the sword what one teaches by the pen is effectively to abandon the prophetic vocation.

There are three points that one should immediately note as part of a larger response here. Firstly, a minor point. Cragg's basic contention is that preaching seeks to persuade, not to impose. But the sinister ring of 'impose' cannot always be contrasted with 'persuade' – for even persuasion can be close to a form of (non-violent) imposition as when, for example, it deliberately appeals to prejudice and irrational sentiment. In that sense, propaganda, advertising – and, on occasion, preaching – can be forms of persuasion that are almost as bad as imposition.

Secondly, Cragg insists that the 'Muhammadan' style of militancy merely frustrates evil – it cannot redeem it. This is an important accusation. Yet it has to be said that the distinction between the *forgiveness* of the will to impiety – a demand common to all theisms – and its *redemption* is in fact a sophistication. I believe that the Christian mechanism for redemption, to the extent that it is coherent, is essentially no different from the ordinary religious demand – common to all theisms – for forgiveness and forbearance. However, if redemption effectively implies passivity in the face of gross injustice, then Christians and Muslims do indeed walk on separate paths for this part of the journey.

The above caveat about coherence is important. There is, I would argue, a residue of human perversity and evil that cannot be, in any coherent metaphysic, 'redeemed'. There is no intelligible move that could possibly accomplish that. The capacity to thwart divine purposes and oppose the prophetic cause is an integral liability of the free human person. And such a capacity generates evil and perversity that cannot always be redeemed in the radical sense intended by Christians. There is no mechanism that can bleach out sin from the human cloth. At best, it can be opposed, subdued, and occasionally forgiven – by God or by His prophetic representative. There are forms of evil which no morally constrained sovereignty can fully redeem. Unredeemed wrongdoing, paradigmatically that of the Devil, is an irreducible residue of history – unless we jettison the integrity of the cosmic struggle between good and evil.

And finally, Cragg sees the prophetic repudiation of coercive power as a corollary of the divine desire to avoid compulsion in matters of religion. (*Muhammad and the Christian*, p. 45). This claim raises deeper theological questions about the nature of the deferred punitive measures against persistent disbelief – measures that are central to the eschatology implicit in traditional theisms. In recent decades, some Christian, mainly Protestant, thinkers have decided to abandon belief in Hell largely because they feel, in the face of secular sensibilities, embarrassed by a 'God of the Fire'. In a characteristic revisionist move, Hell has been eviscerated to a mere feeling of alienation from God – without the physical terrors so evident in the classical portrait. Jesus himself certainly had some harsh things to say about those who rejected him. When the reckoning comes to pass, it is not clear that the God of the Christian scriptures will be as eager as some modern Christian theologians to disown the threat of force and punishment.

6

'The Hijrah is not rightly seen', writes Cragg, 'as a lapse away from prophethood, but as its due sequence of obedience' (*Muhammad and the Christian*, p. 23). This is an equivocal statement – similar to several others at crucial junctures in his arguments – that needs a reading. I interpret it to mean that prophethood came to an end at Mecca and that in Medina Muhammad implemented the purely religious commission he had received in Mecca. Muhammad was, as the Christian Islamicist Montgomery Watt has also insisted, a statesman, not a prophet, in Medina.

Both the view Cragg is here disowning and the view he is upholding are mistaken. The office of prophethood takes the *Hijra* in its stride; it is entirely unaffected by the move. God is as free to reveal His will to powerful men as to powerless ones.

Sustaining Cragg's reservations about the post-*Hijra* ministry is a false, indeed unworthy, ideal of 'success' in matters of faith – an ideal Cragg arbitrarily attributes to Muslim ambition. Cragg insists, without benefit of reason or evidence, that the aim of 'Muhammadan' religion is victory rather than justice and the triumph of a correct ideal. Why can't one aim at both? In fact, the primary concern of Islam is to achieve piety (*taqwa*) on a social as well as individual level. Men are to surrender both individually and communally to the will of God. That is our, human, share in the affair. If God crowns our endeavours with worldly success and a prosperous social order, that is His prerogative. If He doesn't, one bears it patiently. But it is natural to seek success. There is no religious veto on success if it can be worthily and properly attained. A God worthy of reverence would not be the one to render vain our efforts. We have the Koran itself to support us in this confidence.

'There can be no doubt', writes Cragg, rushing in where he should fear to tread, 'that the Prophet's militancy ensured his cause, and ensured its compromise' (*Muhammad and the Christian*, p. 50). What precisely is the compromise here? Does (worldly) success of itself constitute compromise? Does a cause have to fail, then, in order to be authentic? That religion is somehow indifferent, even allergic, to worldly success is a view that may well be seen as a very pardonable prejudice – but a prejudice none the less.

Nor is it the case, notwithstanding Cragg, that the central question here is to do with whether or not moral preaching and political activism, the word and the sword, are compat-

ible. The answer to that question is, in one important
sense, clearly in the affirmative; and Cragg hardly needs
to move outside Christian experience to recognize this as
one possible answer. The proper questions that need to be
posed here are entirely different: is the morally constrained
use of force legitimate? Can armed struggle be a valid part
of religious ambition?

Cragg insists, without adequate argument, that the Islamic concern is solely with political success – at all costs. He
quotes, with approval, Malachi Martin's true but irrelevant
verdict about the need for coercion and power if political
success were to be secured in seventh-century Arabia (and
all this as if Muhammad's Arabia were alone in sustaining
the link between success and power!). The deeper issues
about the essence of Islam are, unsurprisingly, in the
interests of polemical intentions, shelved completely. What
is Islam? Is it a comprehensive system of practice and ideal
reflecting the divine will on earth? Could such a system
reasonably omit the political sphere – itself massively distinctive of human culture? The aim of the Koran is to bring
the existing political order within the purview of the divine
dictate and thereby to purify, sanctify and cleanse it as
much as may be possible. It is difficult to see why such a
desire should be an unworthy one – for God or for us.

7

There is no harm in hoping for success – but what of
failure? What of intractable and large-scale failure, even
tragedy? Surely these are normal casualties in the pursuit
of success. In raising these issues, we also raise the entire
debate on to a much higher level of seriousness. For we
touch here on issues about the character of God, and, in
so doing, on the most fundamental aspects, both doctrinal
and temperamental, of opposed versions of the religious
imagination. Which vision is authentic, truer to the facts
of life and historical experience? Does traditional Islam
have adequate resources to deal with failure and tragedy
in the human world?

Christianity differs from Islam on a matter, fundamental enough, relating to temperament. That temperament, in turn, feeds on opposed doctrines about tragedy in the created order. Cragg often notes that Islam 'lacks' the accents of tragedy and pathos so familiar to readers of the New Testament and the Book of Job in the Old Testament. True enough; but it is a further (and extremely involved) question whether or not this constitutes a deficiency in the implied negative sense. Certainly Islam, as Nietzsche notes in *The Anti-Christ*, is a religious vision that is staunchly opposed to tragedy; and it is fair to say that the greatest ideological achievement of this religion has been its success in effectively reversing and frustrating the will to tragedy – for countless millions – after a deep entrenchment of tragedy within the theistic imagination for centuries. But is it a defect?

We need to shelve this question here. It would be instructive to begin by speculating on the reasons behind the absence of 'tragedy' in the Islamic vision. Cragg puts it pointedly: 'It is fair to ask how the revelation might have been if there had been a Karbalā' inside the Koran' (*Muhammad and the Christian*, p. 144). In the event, the tragedy of Karbalā' – in which a righteous Ḥusayn was martyred by Yazid's forces – occurs in AD 680, well after the close of the koranic revelations. Cragg's enquiry is perceptive, but the Islamic answer is surprisingly simple and surprisingly obvious. The revelation, in its instincts and dominant mood, would have remained identical, absorbing the tragic episode into a larger picture of success and political confidence.

There are, interestingly, a few incidents of worldly failure falling within the period of the revelation of the Koran and hence receiving a mention in the sacred text. None is, of course, quite as traumatic – especially in Shī'a experience – or as far-reaching in consequence as Karbalā' has, sadly, proved to be. Let us take the indecisive battle of Mount Uḥud as an example of inconclusive victory, possibly failure. The Muslims, as in the Battle of Ḥunayn, took keen pleasure in surveying their military prowess. But victory, the Koran warned them, was with God's help alone. And God, whatever Napoleon might say of Him, is not always on the side of the strongest battalion. Owing to a minor act of disobedience by some of the archers protecting the outer flank, who were attracted by the prospect of booty, the Muslims lost a battle that would otherwise have been an even greater success than Badr. After Uhud, the Prophet's camp had to fly their flag at half-mast, for the pagans knew their logic: if Badr was evidence of divine favour, Uhud was evidence of the opposite. Perhaps, after all, the Islamic deity wasn't more powerful than the idols dear to the pagan Quraysh.

The Koran, of course, drew different conclusions. And these are exclusively to do with patience and endurance in the hour of trial. There is no implication that any kind of failure is irreversible or permanent – a central element in any tragic outlook. Optimism wins the day. Indeed, the Koran draws, if we may enlist a discrepant ally, a Nietzschean lesson for the sufferers: 'What does not kill me makes me stronger – lessons from the military school of life' (*Maxims, Twilight of the Idols*). Muhammad himself remained determined; Islam was strong enough to survive the crisis. With much psychological insight, he was out in the field the very next day, still injured and bandaged, but with his army camped within sight of the enemy. The Meccans saw the huge camp-fires blazing for several days and felt, perhaps wrongly, that Muhammad and his followers were still strong enough to win. The tactic had worked.

The lessons of Uhud were quickly learnt. Failure served to broaden perspectives in multiple ways. God meted out those difficult days in order to test and try the mettle of the pious and to honour them by taking martyrs from among them. As for suffering, didn't the pagans suffer too? But the believers were hoping for God's grace denied to rejectors. The only issue here is patience. A chilly hour in June is no more the end of the summer of success than a bright day in December is the end of the winter of discontent. Both success and failure are didactic: Uhud taught what Badr could not. But, in the end, the only cure for failure is success.

There are multiple entailments here relating to the larger issues of the nature of 'success' and 'failure' in matters of the spirit. These are here left aside, having discussed some of them in Chapter 2; but there is one issue, frequently caught up in discussions of tragedy in Islam, which needs to be broached here. This is the problem of the minority instinct in the House of Islam represented by the Shī'a, brought to prominence recently in Iran. Cragg makes much of the tragic dimension of Shī'a history informing an arguably more profound, more pessimistic theology, alert to dimensions of pathos, consuming grief and permanent failure. Unlike the dominant and largely successful Sunnī majority, the Shī'a have a history of minority status within Islamic hegemony and, to some extent, a corresponding history of suffering, particularly in the sad episode of the alleged usurpation of the right of Ali to 'succeed' Muhammad. That sadness was to be compounded by subsequent failures, especially those exemplified in the legacy of tears that up to this day 'celebrates' the consequential martyrdom of Husayn in the Karbalā' massacre perpetrated by nominal Sunnīs against the Prophet's line on that shameful Tenth of Muharram, 680. No witness of this inveterate grief, re-enacted annually in Shī'a passion, can remain unmoved by its telling and melancholy clue to the evil and callousness of a powerful establishment in 'religious' dress.

This is an involved topic that interests me, as a Sunnī, in its own right. For our purposes here, it is enough to note that Cragg misunderstands the significance of suffering in Shī'a thought. For this stream of dissident piety is squarely within the instincts of Islam as far as attitudes towards success and failure are concerned. The notion of tragedy in Cragg's sense has no place in Shī'a thought, whether ancient or contemporary. For Cragg, tragedy typically not only deepens the contemplative spirit in us but also effectively atrophies the will to political activism as one realizes that, in Cragg's phrase, man is not 'politically perfectible' (*Muhammad and the Christian*, p. 48). But any such implication is anathema to Shī‘a thought. After all, Shī‘a Iran has given the contemporary Muslim world its only revolution in the name of God. Can political activism on this dramatic scale find favour in the eyes of those who reject the political dimension as somehow 'shallow' or unworthy of religion? It is noteworthy that, in the modern Middle Eastern context too, only secular political movements such as the PLO feed on tragic perceptions of the human condition. Wherever Islam has had a say, as in the *intifāḍa* in the territories occupied by Israel, there is an almost unaccountable sense of hope and optimism even in severely trying circumstances.

Shī‘a and Sunnī scholars are unanimous that the Koran has an executive function, that it may serve as a guide for administrators. The Medinan state was a landmark in the history of Islam remaining, according to Muslims, to this day the blueprint for a perfect society. Shī‘a theology concurs with Sunnī theology that the apparatus of government should survive the Prophet's demise. The schism between the two traditions is not about the issue of the continuation of Islamic rule but rather about the right person to head the Islamic state. Who should have been at the helm of Muslim political destiny after the Prophet had left the scene? Should it have been Abū Bakr – as Sunnīs aver – or rather the politically unambitious but saintly Ali? That is the central quarrel between the Shī‘a and the Sunnī traditions. Both parties accept the Islamic involvement with power.

8

The Muslim drive for success has a sure koranic warrant. The entire pagan order must be overthrown; and overthrown in the name of God. Within the Koran, there are many calls for struggle in the way of God, for promoting the cause of Islam. To settle for a premature peace – when residues of injustice still taint the order – is condemned as a sign of weakness and cowardice. In the event, virtually nothing of the old Arabian *status quo* was left after Allah and His Messenger had done with it. And what was left suffered a complete transformation as latent pagan energies were systematically released, sublimated and channelled in the service of the new cause. The Koran mercilessly attacked the contemporary sinful society in all its dark detail, ranging from infanticide to indiscriminate atrocities committed against members of alien tribes. Even to call the scriptural onslaught 'revolutionary' is here perhaps to use too lenient a vocabulary; but it is a word with a welcome accent of the Muslims' characteristic commitment to power and polity deployed to sustain justice.

Immediately we need to be careful. It is true that the scripture of Islam is frequently concerned with power and the political. Yet 'political' here is not intended to convey a narrow significance – the modern Western significance of the term. It is not simply a delineation of struggles for place, post and prominence, a jostling for influential positions. The koranic theme is fundamentally different; it has to do with the general subordination of the ways of the world – with their usual overtones of inveterate perversity and opposition to the just cause – to the ways of God, to the ways of a benevolent and just sovereignty. And this reason is sufficient in itself for us to say that if the Koran be political, it is not political in ethos as in 'all's fair in love and war'. This is not to deny that it is partly 'political' – in our narrow sense – with respect to its contents. It is to say, however, that its authorship is motivated by an impulse radically more profound than that designated by the term 'political'. And that deeper impulse is, of course, supplied by the central imperative of all scripture – namely to seek holiness by sanctifying every circumstance of birth and biography, both personal and communal, in the larger hope of God's mercy. This is why Christian and secular critics are wrong in saying that the pursuit of power makes Muslims into fanatics for their cause. Rather, it is the cause of Islam that recruits, harnesses and sanctifies both the 'fanaticism' and the will to success.

In this way, the desecularization of politics has, contrary to popular misconception, resulted in toleration, not bigotry; justice, not caprice. Precisely because theirs was a political creed, Muslims were obliged by the letter of their Law to tolerate their minorities in a way which in Europe, at least before the weakening of Christian values, proved impossible. Hence, for instance, 'no part of the world has been more tolerant in history to its Jewish population than the lands of Islam' (Neil Ascherson, the *Independent on Sunday*, 11 November, 1990). Had Islam renounced politics, the fate of the Jews, Christians and sundry other communities in the Islamic world might well have been very different. The enthusiasm of religion in any devout society will perforce spill over into the political realm, and it is only if that realm is governed by ethical controls grounded in the religion itself that abuses stand any chance of being held in check.

9

Success can corrupt; power is a dangerous thing. Cragg, perhaps mindful of past Christian experiments with religious government, rightly warns Muslims of the dangers of polity, particularly of a theocracy that may degenerate into the worst kind of totalitarianism. Those who claim divine guidance are often reluctant to accept purely human criticism of their policies. Yet such criticism there usually is; and opposition must grow secretly, under the patronage of hypocrisy (*nifāq*) lest it be discerned and challenged. Indeed, the opposition may often have good grounds for their reservations. For rulers often usurp what is a trust from God, what is ultimately God's. The apparatus of government must be accountable both to the community (*umma*) and to God. Yet too often it fails to respect these constraints, elevating itself into a kind of god, an absolute.

All these, Cragg reminds us, are the characteristic menaces of 'political religion'. Islam, paradigmatically a 'political' faith, setting great store by its embracing of power as a means of securing social justice and as an agent of amelioration, must recognize the dangers that power brings in its train.

Fair enough. Nothing that Cragg says here is, of course, alien to the Muslim mind. The Koran itself is fully alert to the dangers of recruiting power 'in the name of God'. There are constant appeals for discrimination and care in the execution of God's designs by fallible human beings. Cragg is not satisfied. Why, he wonders, does the scripture of Islam not show any signs of a radical diffidence about the truth and validity of its cause? (*Muhammad and the Christian*, pp. 132–3.) Why were the early Muslims, he wonders *in the same breath*, significantly, so confident that their cause and God's cause coincided exactly? Cragg's own answer is, predictably, that a faith lacking in emphases on failure and tragedy is liable to attract votaries who are hasty both in their confidence and in their militancy.

There are two distinct worries here, though Cragg writes as if these were aspects of a single concern. With respect to the Koran's own confidence, it is fair to say that *all* sacred literature in the Hebrew tradition tends to be aristocratic in mood. God asserts; He does not argue. God, as morally and metaphysically perfect, has no reason to doubt the righteousness of His cause. Cragg's probing here betrays prejudicial rigour. It is true of course that, for Cragg, the Koran is not the Word of God but rather the product of fallible human authorship. But it is equally true that the Koran itself does not proceed on Cragg's presuppositions.

The confidence of Muslim believers is another matter altogether. Cragg conflates the confidence of the author of the Koran with the confidence of Muslim readers. The worry about the believers' conviction has a different status; and it is indeed a very significant concern in the political life. This is why devout Muslims have always placed great emphasis on interiority of motive and purity of intention when engaged in *jihād* on behalf of God. The Koran itself is well aware of the manner in which men usurp priorities and rights not properly their own. Did the early Muslims too readily identify their own interests with those of their God? Did they really strive for the establishment of Islam or for their personal gain? It is difficult for anyone tolerably well-informed of the history of early Islam to retain a choice in answering these questions. But to everyone alike is the right to conscience in matters of moment.

That there are Muslims today, as there have been throughout history, who prostitute Islam in the service of purely personal or national interests is entirely undeniable. Do they really mean *Allāhu akbar* in their rallies? (Or is it, in the latest fashion, just a way of challenging Westerners?) That individuals and whole nations can cynically exploit Islam is surely not at issue. And it is here that one needs to restrain one's judgements, especially as an outsider, and bear in mind the failings of our common humanity.

10

Once [a] man came to see me while I was lying in prison . . .
He said: 'Politics is all dirt, lying, and viciousness; why don't you leave it to us?' What he said was true in a sense; if that is what politics really consists of, it belongs exclusively to them.

Ayatollah Khomeini goes on predictably to contrast the politics of Islam and the Muslims as morally constrained, subject to the dictates of revealed scripture (*Selected Sayings of Ayatollah al-Khomeini*, Islamic Centre, Stanmore, 1989, p. 30). It is this latter kind of politics that necessarily demands the engagement of Muslims – unless, of course, they wish to abdicate their responsibilities as citizens.

It is no doubt true that the political life has a tendency to degenerate easily into a pursuit of ends that are not, either in design or inception, moral in quality. Given that the struggle for power has been and remains intense among all of us, including those who claim no interest in the benefits of that facility, it would be odd if there were no moral risks involved. There is a pronounced tension between the purity of motive demanded by the religious life, on the one hand, and the need for diplomacy and forceful sanction so central and necessary to life in a corrupt world, on the other. Yet there is no way out of this one. Social reformers, such as the Prophet of Islam, having embraced power, can merely do their best in ensuring that, in terms of the establishment of socially just institutions, the benefits of dirtying one's hands are greater than the benefits of keeping them clean. In the last analysis, this may well be a choice between evils; but it is not a choice concerning which one can plead indifference, let alone immunity.

This coin has, happily, another and very encouraging side too. An acceptance of the need to enact the faith in social forms enables the average believer to put his words into action. And action is, as all wisdom unanimously teaches, more salutary than mere idle hopes and wishes felt in some fugitive mood at the close of day. It is true that such action may be, on occasion, wrongly motivated or have disastrous consequences. But inaction never fails in either respect. We, as ordinary men and women, need realistic ideals, enjoining appropriate action, to exhaust allegiance; we are not in need of impossible ideals that are merely an embarrassing reminder of our own imperfections – especially imperfections of which we are only too aware and indeed all the more aware for failing to eliminate.

The only genuine alternative to power is political daydreaming. There are in the world today, as critics of Islam's militancy well know, many familiar varieties of unwarrantable cheerfulness fed on a diet of supposed personal salvation, a private rescue from public distress. Such private solace fosters a facility which always serves to carry its possessors very lightly through the indifference and cruelty of the real world. Indeed it dulls the pain that men of goodwill necessarily feel when contemplating the vast panorama of contemporary evil follies, perverse fanaticisms, and militant oppositions to the good and the just. But the liabilities of private salvation are fully displayed in the hour of practical action. To perfect oneself, to secure one's own salvation and that of one's own little club is only to cut the first sod. There is still the vast and untended field of duties to the world and to the larger community of man.

11

Warning without sanction virtually never suffices to remove injustice. As every student of history, modern and ancient, well knows, establishments are never eager to effect just reforms that would curtail the existing interests secured by an unjust order. (Think here of modern South Africa.) The task of the political reformer – be he Moses, Muhammad or Marx – is therefore to assess the liabilities of an improper use of power *and* the benefits of a proper recruitment of that facility. This is the real issue here. The view that power should never be recruited, that all its employments are necessarily wrong, is the kind of subtlety best left for academic exchange in the footnotes of Christian theology journals. Meanwhile, in the real world, we know that all cultures, including Christian ones, instinctively seek (and occasionally enjoy) the sanction of political power. The only relevant task therefore is to make its employment legitimate – in turn by qualifying authority, that is, making it rational, discriminating, and morally constrained.

It is one of Islam's signal achievements as a revelation to have recognized the indispensability of power in a world that perennially harbours the impulse to militant impiety. This Islamic insight is the natural, indeed inevitable, result of holding one's eyes and ears close to the texture of life, by making thoughtful contact with the true nature of human perversity empowered by the establishment. It is a recognition that is sound, inspired as it is by a correct verdict about the *actual* relationship between ideal and reality, between demand and the will to submission.

Faith is as faith does; and it can do little without the power that can protect its heritage and ensure its future. A recognition of the indispensability of power alters the whole nature of this debate. At best, the critic can quarrel with Muhammad's actual politics; he can hardly censure his attempt to recruit the political. Muhammad was a politician-prophet. He had a genius for diplomacy and the calculating realism of politics; his attempt to subdue the

Quraish and unite the Arab tribes was part of a master-plan executed with astonishing precision and foresight. That political career, like any other, is subject to moral appraisal.

And yet such an appraisal itself must take the full measure of the Prophet's achievement of professed religious ends. The propriety (or otherwise) of his recruitment of the political arm cannot be exclusively assessed on *a priori* grounds nor on exterior theological bases that beg the question against the Islamic pattern of piety.

Muhammad, unlike some other seminal religious figures, risked his reputation for personal holiness by soiling his hands with the political muck. (Merely to seek personal purity can also be a form of selfishness – albeit one superior to most varieties.) It was a great and heroic risk; he succeeded. The 'Islamic Revolution' in Medina was the least violent in all of history, with barely a hundred casualties. There is here no love of violence; believers are, as the Koran instructs them, 'to enter fully into peace [*silm*]' (Koran 2: 208). (Peace, incidentally, is one of the root meanings of the word *islām*.) The Prophet soberly recognized that in a world addicted to the logic of coercion, negotiation with evil sometimes needs to be supplemented with a confrontation in the sphere of physical power. Force, moreover, can sometimes be the tool of a certain kind of diplomacy based on deterrence.

To be sure, none of this is to deny the very real dangers and pitfalls of the political life. To cultivate the right spirit in which political tasks should be undertaken is an obligation transparent in the Koran's ethics. For the sacred volume is concerned to take the political temper and, like all else in life, recruit it for a comprehensively religious vocation. Cragg's fundamental point, severely Protestant in complexion, wholly out of touch with the realities of ancient history as well as recent memory, is that the very recruitment of the political, irrespective of its potential legitimacy, is a sufficient reason for 'an inescapable reservation of heart' about Muhammad's style of religion. It is a judgement at once too absolute and trapped in a vision that sets itself needlessly insoluble problems. Cragg's words are in need of being softened by the qualifications that experience, political practice, and history jointly bring. Only within the laudable realism of Islam does the rendering unto Caesar of the things that are Caesar's become not the false antithesis – as in Christian reflection – but rather the true measure of rendering unto God the things that are God's.

12

'Purify the heart – and the institutions will follow.' Do they? Why not: 'Purify the institutions – and the heart will follow?' But a just order is impossible without collective purity of heart. True enough; but a pure individual heart is no bulwark against an unjust order. Cragg's dispute with Islamic verdicts on the relationship between social power and individual conscience is, as part of a larger debate, rather topical these days. It is as well to broaden perspectives here, if only briefly. For the current debate on social justice is also bedevilled by the same question about the correct balance between the reform of individual hearts and the structural changes that, variously, presuppose such a reform or are themselves the cause of it. There is a kind of Christian approach to problems of social injustice which identifies the correct procedure with a change of individual hearts – along with the attendant hope that the world will change in consequence. And there is the opposed strategy, popular with Marxists, of laying one's bet on changing structures and then hoping for a change in the individual's heart – the latter usually being considered superfluous in a structurally perfect world. Both views, expressed here very crudely but not unfairly, are mistaken. Clearly, we need to change both men's hearts and the power structures that lodge and perpetuate injustice. It is this reasoning, no doubt, that was impressed upon the Prophet as he set out to establish the foundation of the Medinan polity.

Christian thinkers typically tend to place the emphasis firmly on the need to reform the heart and conscience.

Some among them, usually those with socialist leanings, may see this as a preface to structural changes. But, given the reservation about the 'political perfectibility of man', in Cragg's phrase, most Christian thinkers do not believe we can have a Utopia this side of the grave. At best, then, we can have individual piety within a social order that need not respect Christian constraints.

Now, it is true, of course, as Christians always remind Muslims, that 'law does not change the heart'. But it is equally true, as Martin Luther King reminds all of us, that 'it does restrain the heartless'. And it is this latter emphasis on the need to protect the rights of the poor and weak which is so marked a feature of Muslim thought. It is true that some Christians, particularly those confronted with real situations of injustice, rather than theorizing from a comfortable distance, have also recently developed a 'liberation theology' in Third World contexts; but such theology has as yet received little backing from orthodoxy. Muslims, by contrast, have always opted for a firm emphasis on the need for laws and political mechanisms, revolutionary if required, that protect us from each other's callousness and avarice. With their comparatively optimistic and positive view of human nature (a view which rejects the doctrine of original sin as unjust and superfluous), Muslims teach that the religious soul is capable of struggling against injustice without being fatally tempted by the darker possibilities of power. It is because Islam regards the political sphere as theoretically possible of redemption, or even as an arena for renunciation and self-purification, that it attempts to redeem it. But this kind of humanism is surely foreign to the Christian mind: Samuel Johnson was, uncharacteristically, wrong when he mused:

How small of all that human hearts endure
That part which laws or Kings can cause or cure.

Powerlessness is a demoralizing experience. Apolitical religion itself can easily corrode the hearts of religious men, who feel obliged to stand back, merely wringing their hands when confronted with the spectacle of oppression.

What, the Muslim wonders, can have been the inner state of the Lutheran bishops who refused to struggle against Hitler's régime? Can one compromise so fully with evil, and still be capable of prayer? It is for the modern Christian to explain to the world how such a conjunction might be imaginable, let alone achieved.

13

The reader may well have developed a sense that we are gradually moving away from a defence of the Islamic involvement with power to an attack on the modern Christian desire to remain aloof from political ambition. Such a reader would be right. For I do believe that in the interests of fairness, Christianity too must face the tribunal of accusation here. There has been a marked tendency among Christians to entertain triumphalist sentiments with respect to the Muslim involvement with power. Christians, then, are undefiled by the muck of political life, while Muslims, particularly 'fundamentalists', are only too eager to dirty their hands. Should such a stance go unchallenged?

'The distinction that really matters,' writes George Orwell in his essay 'Lear, Tolstoy and the Fool', 'is not between violence and non-violence, but between having and not having the appetite for power' (*Inside the Whale and Other Essays*, Harmondsworth: Penguin, 1957, p. 118). This perceptive remark contains the germ of our criticism here. Anyone who has moved in Muslim activist circles will have heard the story of the caliph Ali, who, in the heat of battle, was about to deliver the *coup de grâce* to a knight from the enemy host, but who, when the man spat in his face, stayed his hand, aware that the believer must kill only for righteousness' sake, free of every personal rancour and will for vengeance.

The Sufi writer Frithjof Schuon is also concerned with this stress on intention:

'Judge not that ye be not judged . . .'; 'All they that take the sword shall perish by the sword . . .'; 'Whichsoever of you is without sin, let him cast the first stone . . .' None of these

sayings is explicable unless we take account of the
characteristic intention which lies behind them, namely, that
they are addressed, not to man as such, but to man under the
sway of passion, or else to the passional (*sic*) side of man. For
it is plainly evident that it can and must happen that one man
should pass a legitimate judgement upon another, but for which
there should be neither 'discernment of spirits' nor justice; or
that men should draw the sword rightly without therefore
perishing by the sword, or again that men should cast stones
if need be without being compelled to ask themselves whether
or not they are sinners, for it goes without saying that neither
judges nor executioners have to ask themselves this question
in the course of exercising their respective functions. To
confront the Laws of Sinai or those of the Quran and the
Sunnah with those of Christ is not to establish a contradiction,
but simply to speak of different things.

(F. Schuon, *Islam and the Perennial Philosophy* [London:
World of Islam Festival Publishing Co., 1976], p. 18.)

Orwell himself continues, in a long passage whose lesson
for the Christian conscience could hardly be clearer:

There are people who are convinced of the wickedness both of
armies and of police forces, but who are nevertheless much
more intolerant and inquisitorial in outlook than the normal
person who believes that it is necessary to use violence in
certain circumstances. They will not say to somebody else, 'Do
this, that and the other or you will go to prison', but they
will, if they can, get inside his brain and dictate his thoughts
for him in the minutest particulars. Creeds like pacifism and
anarchism, which seem on the surface to imply a complete
renunciation of power, rather encourage this habit of mind.
For if you have embraced a creed which appears to be free
from the ordinary dirtiness of politics – a creed from which
you yourself cannot expect to draw any material advantage –
surely that proves that you are in the right? And the more
you are in the right, the more natural that everyone else should
be bullied into thinking likewise. (Orwell, *op. cit.*, p. 118.)

Modern Christianity can certainly be classified here along
with pacifism and anarchism. For all three are united in
their tendency to claim a repudiation of political power.
Muslims care about power and dispassionately seek it.

But Islamic doctrine regulates what in Christian thought is happily ignored or disowned.

14

If Islam despises Christianity, it is a thousand times right to do so. Islam presupposes men . . .

The writer of these harsh words is not some contemporary Muslim apologist relishing Islam's laudable realism about human nature and the social order. It is in fact the German philosopher Friedrich Nietzsche in his iconoclastic *The Anti-Christ* (Penguin edition, p. 183). Nietzsche is here discussing and commending Islamic candour about the frailties of men and women and, relatedly, of the need for ideals that take account of such weaknesses.

Islam certainly presupposes human beings – ordinary, fallible, human, all too human. And the involvement with power is, as Christian critics rightly insist, characteristic of Islam. But isn't it similarly true of all viable ideologies? Perhaps Muslims are frank about their willingness to employ force, duly constrained by moral scruple derived from religious revelation. Perhaps Christians lack candour here. Nor will it do to say that Christianity, unlike Islam, does not incorporate the political wing into its original self-definition. One is still validly concerned with the actual Christian interpretation of that disavowal, with the behaviour of Christians within the hurly-burly of history. What Christianity actually is in recent and ancient history is no less interesting and relevant here than the 'perfect' Christianity formed by the impulses of modern idealism and romanticism smuggled backwards, so to speak, into its alleged origins. No religion whose votaries have conquered much of the globe in the hope of saving others (and presumably themselves) can be entitled to claim the privilege of a fundamental indifference to power – unless, of course, one indulges a private sense of humour. Official Christianity has often endorsed a particular style of management of subjugated peoples, a style marked by an unremitting search for unfair privilege. Whole nations have been impoverished so that a tiny irreligious and corrupt élite can continue to milk resources and maintain itself in a position of undeserved affluence. And if one tries to get off the hook by conceding that the behaviour of these colonialist Christians is an improper interpretation of the cause of Jesus of Nazareth, then that fact too is revealing – whether as a melancholy commentary on the radical failings of Christian humanity or as a vital clue to the futility of impossibly difficult ideals, or both.

It cannot be denied that the Christian faith has in the past regularly sought authority over the powers temporal. And Muslims today have no particular reason to regard modern Christian attitudes, demonstrably influenced by their liberal-secular backdrop, as any more authentic than medieval Catholic and Byzantine theologies which assumed the involvement with politics to be a moral imperative. The whole history of the medieval papacy reveals the Christian need to be bound up with the political realm, in an attempt to sanctify it. (It might be concluded, in the interests of constructive dialogue, that the Muslim quarrel here is with certain threads within Christian thought which have lately gained prominence, and not with the Christianity of the great ages of faith.)

Social and political reality, not eager to reflect the slogans of Christian apology, leave a lot to be desired. Official Christianity has tended, and still does in many contexts, to abet and second cruelty and injustice. South Africa is an obvious example of a country where the Christian creed has been used, or rather prostituted, to legitimize oppression. But the Christian stance on power readily lends itself to such misuse. Passivity in the face of gross injustice is, as Marxists rightly tell us, in need of elaborate justification. It is morally much more acceptable to opt for a constrained use of force. The oppressed man, waging his daily struggle, needs plenty of patience if his attempt to recruit force against blatant injustice is made conditional on the supply of a coherent Christian theology authorizing its employment.

Western Christians often congratulate themselves on

their renunciation of power, their refusal to embrace the political arm. Yet in the pursuit of justice, it is, tragically, often necessary to have bloody hands. And, given the kind of world we live in, clean hands are often a far better indication of callousness of heart than bloody ones. There is no doctrine more congenial to tyrants than a religion which claims no political entailments.

The whole image of power, within the Christian imagination, needs careful re-assessment in the twentieth century. For most Christians and pacifists, power conjures up the images of Orwell's political masterpiece *Nineteen Eighty-four*. There is the rubber truncheon wielded by hooded guards, the huge iron boot descending on the upturned, defenceless face, networks of barbed wire, and so on. And yet this is, of course, the ethos not only of power but of powerlessness. It all depends on which side of the barbed wire one is on.

Let's stay with Orwell awhile. What he, rightly, opposed was the abuse of power as men indulged in doublethink – became intellectually and morally lazy. But such moral slackness is an attitude precisely opposed to the exacting reflection (*tadabbur*) of the Koran. Power can certainly become an end in itself – as it does in the police-state of *Nineteen Eighty-four*. But the lesson here cannot be that power should be completely renounced.

There is an evident implausibility in the black Christian posture of non-violence in a country such as South Africa. To renounce the facility of force in such a struggle against an unjust order is itself morally absurd. And it is, notwithstanding Christian apology, an absurdity no religious sanction can sanctify. One has every right to remind the oppressed to imitate Christ in his suffering and powerlessness. But this can at best be an occasional act of supererogation, not a routine demand of social behaviour. It may be fine to turn the other cheek. But where other people's cheeks are being slapped, we are surely obliged to intervene.

Muslims cannot endorse the Christian attitude of effective passivity in the face of gross injustice. Nor should the

Muslim conscience feel in any way inhibited in its militant opposition to injustice – by the, let us say, reproachful verdicts of modern Christians who implicate Islamic doctrine as encouraging gratuitous belligerence.

15

It is legitimate to suspect that present Christian unease about 'political religion' has been informed by specifically European experiences of theocracy. Most notoriously since the Reformation, religion acting in sanction of kingships has inspired some of the continent's most damaging wars. Additionally, much contrite recognition is now being made of the extent to which religious fervour contributed to some of the worst excesses of colonialism. Towards conquered unbelievers the teachings of the Church had usually been unmistakable:

With the coming of Christ every office and all governmental authority and all lordship and jurisdiction was taken from every infidel lawfully and with just cause, and granted to the faithful through Him who has the supreme power and cannot err.

The passage is from a perfectly respectable canon lawyer of the thirteenth century, cited in James Muldoon, *Popes, Lawyers and Infidels: The Church and the Non-Christian World 1250–1550* (Liverpool University Press, 1979, p. 16).

Ironically, Muslim societies (which forgive, but sometimes find it hard to forget) have borne the brunt of aggression directly sponsored by the Church: the Crusades and the Inquisition being only the most disturbing examples. Here, for instance, is a characteristic voice of medieval Catholicism, culled from the bull *Romanus Pontifex*, dated 1454, in which Pope Nicholas V gives Alfonso V of Portugal the right

to invade, search out, capture, vanquish, and subdue all Saracens and pagans whatsoever, and other enemies of Christ wherever they live, along with their kingdoms, dukedoms, principalities, lordships and goods, both chattels and real estate, that they hold and possess . . . to reduce their persons

to perpetual slavery and to take for himself and his heirs their
kingdoms . . .

(cited in Muldoon, p. 134)

And in South America, this is how Christian outreach
tended to proceed:

The *Requerimiento* [a short doxology] contained a statement of
Christian beliefs and an explanation of the Spanish presence
in the Americas. Before troops launched an attack on infidels,
a priest was to read the document to them. Critics from Las
Casas to the present have been scandalized by the vision of a
friar reading this statement to an audience composed of trees
or empty huts, or hurling its words at the backs of fleeing,
uncomprehending Indians, terrified by the sight of armed
strangers. There is no evidence that the text was ever translated
into any American tongue so that the natives might have some
opportunity to understand it.

(Muldoon, p. 140)

And again:

The Conquistadors came as rapacious aggressors, fully
supported by the Church, and with remarkable rapidity took
over the major part of the continent, destroying great
civilisations and eliminating with savagery any groups who
resisted them. The Church for the most part devoted its
energies to mass conversions, often at the point of a sword.

(Duncan Forrester, *Theology and Politics*, Oxford: Basil
Blackwell, 1988, p. 67)

And so on. Given Europe's deplorable record of religious
intolerance, it is hard not to sympathize with those post-
Enlightenment theologians who have feared to tread the
corridors of power.

But what of other, non-European traditions? Has everyone been quite this unpleasant? Is it not the case that
Christianity, made exclusivist by its doctrine of the Incarnation, has tended to take a more hostile view of other
faiths than religions which regard themselves as the best,
but not the only, paths to salvation? Further, does not the
existence of an infallible interpreter in the guise of the
Church tend to foster rigidity and provide a mechanism

for inquisition? We need not go into the implications of these questions here. Suffice it to remark that medieval Muslim society was, in comparison with the Christendom with which it marched, remarkably tolerant both towards dissident Muslims and to confessional minorities. There are, of course, instances of persecutions and heresy trials, but one looks in vain for an equivalent to what one may fairly term the genocidal instinct which broke surface with such frequency in Christian lands.

It was this very tolerance of the Islamic dispensation, a needful one given its 'eschatological' position in the world's religious history, which made its rapid expansion possible. An agnostic historian takes up the matter:

The conduct of the caliph Umar at Jerusalem shows us the mildness with which the Arab conquerors treated the vanquished, and contrasts vividly with the actions of the Crusaders in the same city several centuries later. Umar wanted to enter the Holy City with only a small number of his companions. He asked the patriarch Sophronius to accompany him on the visit which he wished to make to the sites consecrated by religious tradition, and then declared to the inhabitants that they were safe, that their property and churches would be respected, and that the Muslims would not make their prayers in Christian churches.

Amr's conduct in Egypt was no less benign. To its inhabitants he offered complete religious freedom, impartial justice for all, the inviolability of property, and the replacement of the arbitrary and excessive taxes of the Greek emperors by an annual tribute fixed af fifteen dirhams per capita. The inhabitants of the provinces showed themselves so satisfied with these offers that they lost no time in agreeing to the treaty, and paid the tribute in advance. So religiously did the Arabs respect the conventions which were accepted, so agreeable did they make themselves to the populations which earlier had been subjected to the vexations of the Christian agents of the emperor at Constantinople, that all Egypt adopted their religion and their language with enthusiasm. This, it must be reiterated, was a result which could not have been achieved through force. Not one of the peoples who had ruled Egypt before the Arabs had accomplished this.

(G. Le Bon, *La Civilisation des Arabes*, cited in R. Du Pasquier, *Unveiling Islam*, p. 68)

And again:

The Arabic conquest showed great gentleness toward the Christian population in the subjugated countries. The Christian churches could hardly complain. In AD 650 the head of the Nestorian church was able to write: 'These Arabs do not only avoid fighting Christianity, they even endorse our religion, they honour our priests and holy men and donate gifts to monasteries and churches.

(Tor Andrae, *In the Garden of Myrtles: Studies in Early Islamic Mysticism* (State University of New York Press, 1987), p. 8)

Islam's concern to sanctify the political dimension of human experience can be shown to have underpinned the tolerance and humanity characteristic of its history. By enforcing the juridical principle of *dhimma*, the protection of monotheistic communities enshrined in the teaching of the Prophet, it created a haven not only for its own religious communities, but also for religious refugees of all kinds fleeing from Christian Europe. When Catholicism was reimposed in Andalusia, most Jews chose to emigrate to the Islamic lands rather than remain under Christian rule. And it does not need much imagination to speculate on what might have been the fate of minorities, including, of course, the Eastern Christians, had medieval Muslims left politics to the secular rulers.

Just as the traditional Christian experience of religious government has often been a negative one, so the modern Muslim experience of secular administration has been even worse. Under the Ottoman régime, which was essentially an Islamic order, the Middle East experienced no major conflict for four hundred years, from 1517 to 1917. It is secular modernity, imposed in an endless variety of forms, which, since 1917, has presided over the unrest for which the area is now so notorious.

16

'Muslim activism in struggling to establish a divinely willed society,' writes Father Thomas Michel (in *Salaam*, Vol. 10, No. 2, April 1989, published in New Delhi, p. 74), 'contrasts with Christian emphasis on love, forgiveness, conscience, and the transforming power of suffering "for the sake of justice".' But why the contrast? Can't Muslims also emphasize love, forgiveness, conscience, and so on? Can't Christians also struggle to establish the Kingdom of God on earth? Isn't justice the first public (or structural) priority of private (or religious) confession? In a just society, private virtues (such as individual generosity to the poor) become virtually superfluous. At any rate, no amount of personal generosity can resolve the structural problems of a society based on unjust distributions of power and wealth.

The Koran's verdict is of course unequivocal. 'God has sent down the Book and the balance in order that men may do justice.' A typical verdict from the sacred text (Koran 57:25). The term translated as 'to do justice' (*li-yaqūm al-nāsu bi'l-qisṭ*) has resonances of 'to rise up to justice'. The original language here conceals a revealing hint about Islamic priorities. The preaching, the individual's private sense of right and wrong – all this is prior and preparatory. One reads scripture, learns its demands, purifies the heart in order that one may do – rise up to do – justice.

Elsewhere too, famously and sharply in *Sūra* 107, the Koran condemns those who divorce religious observance from an implied practical concern for the poor and dispossessed. Fulfilling the obligations of koranic piety (in the narrow sense of prayer and fasting) is not an end in itself. The preacher who is content with preaching piety for the private sector is indeed inviting the charge of mere rhetoric.

17

At the height of the Rushdie affair, a Christian acquaintance who endorses Cragg's critique of political religion
complained to me: 'I do wish Muslims would learn to
develop a theology of powerlessness. We did – a long time
ago. With God, nothing succeeds – like failure.'

With God, perhaps; but in the human, all too human,
world, as my Christian acquaintance knew well enough,
the slogan is entirely different. Islam, like any other system
of ideas, including Christianity, instinctively desires and
sometimes secures the sanction of political power. Muslims
have never developed a theology of powerlessness; the
Prophet himself only left a legacy of undiluted success. For
the House of Islam, like any other human solidarity, aims,
among other things, at acquiring power. If it fails, one is
patient. The only cure for failure is success.

It is interesting, incidentally, that the Muslim experience
in the political life has been exactly opposite in character
to much of Jewish experience. While Muslims have never
historically had reason to develop a 'theology of powerlessness', Jewish thinkers have not, since the collapse of the
ancient kingdom of Israel, had reason to develop a theology of power. In recent decades, the House of Islam
has come to encompass many stateless Muslim minorities
whose practice of Islam lacks political establishment. Conversely, the Jewish people in modern Israel have, for the
first time since the collapse of David's kingdom, a state
whose official character is, in some sense, Jewish.

The Prophet, of course, to get back to our story, succeeded; but failure was always a possibility. Cragg is convinced that the *Hijra* and its sequel were necessitated by
lack of success in the Prophet's 'verbal' campaign against
the Meccan idolators. For if the Meccan ministry had led
to a winning of the pagan heart, a retrieval of the perverse
mentality, why the move to Medina? Fair enough. If it had
been God's will that the Quraish willingly embrace Islam,
the actual historical sequence of exile and triumphant
return would not have transpired. Yet the crucial issue

here is hardly historical. It is conceptual: can any adequate definition of Islam omit a reference to the 'power' dimension which the Prophet himself and hence all generations of Muslims since have seen as integral?

This particular question is addressed, if obliquely, in Cragg's discussion of statehood in Islamic political thought – a theme running through his many writings from the early *The Call of the Minaret* (first published in 1956, reissued in 1986 by Collins) to his latest *Readings in the Qur'an* (Collins, 1988). It is a stimulating enquiry; we cannot here do justice to its nuances, but it would be a serious omission to ignore it completely.

In the final chapter of *Jesus and the Muslim*, there occurs a passage in which Cragg makes an uncharacteristic concession to Muslim criticism. For in it Cragg seems to qualify his usual, thoroughly unrealistic, stance on power. 'To diagnose the religious blight of statehood . . .', he writes, 'is not to deny the inevitability of the political order' (*Jesus and the Muslim*, p. 281). He goes on to concede, what is entirely undeniable, that all human solidarities, religious or secular, naturally seek, and sometimes enjoy, the sanction of political power. Yet this is precisely what modern Christians, including Cragg himself, typically deny in polemical exchange – when they are putting their faith on display for the benefit of outsiders. Cragg notes that the Jewish people have recently sought to empower their faith in the precarious Middle East. He also implies, rather weakly perhaps, that Christians too, particularly in the Middle East, have never been unaware of the benefits of power. But, continues Cragg, it is the *temper*, self-critical or otherwise, of these religio-political institutions that is the subject of our proper religious enquiry and, if appropriate, reservation.

Fair enough; but Cragg then provocatively singles out Islam for its (supposed) view of the state as an end in itself (*op cit*. pp. 281ff). Muslims are, he suggests, committed, with a Machiavellian callousness, to the state and worldly success at all costs. Now, one need not even press to fine detail the rhetoric here in order to discern the falsity of

Cragg's claims. That such a view of Islam is demonstrably mistaken should occasion no surprise; what *is* surprising is that a student of Cragg's profound multi-lingual scholarship should, at a crucial juncture, fall victim to partisan sensibility. Such a circumstance is at once witness to the depth of confusion about the essence of Islam and to the powerful hold of certain specifically post-Enlightenment Christian convictions about the nature of true religion as excluding the political wing.

Let's turn directly to Cragg's point. That religious individuals, enjoying the benefit of power, have no great wish to be self-critical is evidently often the case. But as much can be said of any ideological solidarity, religious or secular, enjoying powerful sanction. In any case, the demand for a tolerant and self-accusatory temper is itself a religious, indeed a thoroughly Islamic one.

Certainly, Islam has always seen the state as subordinate to the demands of (revealed) faith. There can be no question of ultimacy for the political establishment. The devotion of the Muslim conscience can have no terminus other than God. Ultimate allegiances cannot be satisfied with verdicts about derivative realities. The object of our devotion is God, not the state that enacts His laws. *Allāhu akbar* is the slogan. Where polity compromises piety, the former must be taken to task. For the piety that demands a polity for the full expression of religious conviction is none the less capable of subordinating and disciplining the state when it betrays the intentions for which it was created. The political life is not autonomous; it is subject to the higher rules of faith.

For Cragg, Muslims wrongly allow religion to be co-extensive with the political establishment. He believes that there is much wisdom in the post-Enlightenment ideal of church-state separation. The truly religious conscience, he argues, does not seek power. In fact, for the Christian, a fully secular statehood is to be welcomed for it provides '. . . an invitation to a humbler posture on the part of religion, a call to serve society from within and not from above' (*The Pen and the Faith*, London: George Allen and Unwin, 1985, p. 6). But can the humility of religious traditions safeguard us against the pride that finds alternative secular sources? It may well be true that the secularization of the state offers religious ambition the suitably modest role of voluntary charitable service. But where the secular state patronizes oppression and injustice, can a religion with so narrow and humble a function effectively oppose it?

There are further and wider implications of this debate. Two deserve a brief mention. Firstly, implicit in Cragg's recommendation of secular statehood is an unjustifiably optimistic estimate of the amenability of secular solidarities to moral constraints. The view that secular postures of power lead to humility in matters of statecraft is certainly questionable in an age that has witnessed the arrogant brutality of two 'world' (or rather 'European') wars, Hiroshima, and the shadow of nuclear holocaust. Virtually all the major tragedies of the twentieth century – possibly mankind's worst century so far – have been caused by secular and nationalist ambitions. The hubris of secularity when it rejects any liability to forces greater than itself is not the more pardonable because its source is not religious. It is well to remember that Orwell's *Nineteen Eighty-four* is a critique of totalitarianism in secular dress. Big Brother was not the Pope or an Ayatollah. Inquisitions are not the monopoly of religious enthusiasms.

Secondly, there is no reason why the possibility of humility in the political ethos cannot obtain within the theocratic pattern of government. Humility and self-critical temperaments are not the exclusive property of secular forms of polity. Indeed, theocracy is a pattern of government that is, when properly implemented, under the aegis of the most radical form of humility. (Think here of the second Caliph, Umar, who was found by the Byzantine ambassador sleeping in the mosque portico, dressed in rags.) That any given form of polity will deteriorate once hubris strikes alliance with the will to arbitrary power is undeniable. The human potential for abusing power is not fully constrained by any form of polity; the will to corruption can safely be expected to create its own circumstance. The political nursery is not the best place for nurturing the moral virtue of humility – although Muslim history affords many instances of successful combinations of the ordeal of politics with the process of self-denial, aided by the recognition that God alone is great. Emir 'Abd al-Qādir of Algeria, who combined ceaseless warfare against the invading French with the so-called 'greater *jihād*' – the war against the lower self – is one outstanding example.

Cragg rightly notes that there are now sizeable Muslim minorities without a state – as in India, Palestine, Kashmir and Europe. He is also right in insisting that Islam can survive without a state – a truth, in any case, amply indicated by the fact that there is, possibly Iran apart, not a single Islamic state in the contemporary world. But his inferences about the pioneering role of a stateless and domesticated Islam in places such as India are a little self-indulgent, betraying as they do details of a distinctively Christian manifesto. He wrongly suggests that such an Islam, devoid of the sanctions of power, will teach Muslims greater humility in the political life. In this connection, he quotes, with approval, the confused verdict of a certain Indian writer, Hasan Askari. Askari's startling claim that the Prophet of Islam did not found a state at all (*Muhammad and the Christian*, p. 49, quoted by Cragg) is demonstrably unhistorical – a piece of baseless speculation that discredits both its author and those who pretend to believe it. Lest parody be suspected or credibility challenged, I quote directly:

My deep conviction is that the Prophet of Islam did not create a state. Consequently, the controversy between Sunni and Shi'ah over the question of knowing who should succeed the Prophet is without foundation. It follows, too, that the principles having to do with the Caliphate and the Imamate are not Quranic. I believe that Islam can survive without political power, without a state.

What a stateless Islam really teaches Muslims is a lesson about something much more time-honoured than humility in politics. It teaches them the liabilities of weakness. Powerlessness corrupts, and absolute powerlessness corrupts absolutely. It is no coincidence that many powerless Muslims have, in their desperation, resorted to political violence and 'terrorism'. Powerful people don't need to hijack aeroplanes or become what cynical newscasters call 'suicide bombers'.

18

Islam in Muslim reflection is the religion of the pen, Muslims a people of the pen. It is significant that the inaugural revelation in *Sūra* 96 (v. 4) already makes a reference to this. The act of reading is the primal act of faith: 'Read!' demands the Angel at Ḥīra. And *Sūra* 68 takes its title from a reference to the pen (*qalam*), seen in the koranic world as the primary symbol of the divine tuition of mankind through the essentially literary institutions of messengership and scripture. For Muslims, the Koran remains the supreme achievement of the divine pen; Islam prides itself on being an intellectual faith *par excellence* which takes its basic definition from the unique literary miracle of the Arabic Koran. Throughout the history of Islam, the initial koranic emphasis on literacy and scholarship has been transparent in the ardent Muslim desire for seeking knowledge – and all as part of a paradigmatically religious obligation. There have been also the auxiliary arts of the pen – calligraphy most notably – in which much Muslim ambition has been invested.

Outside Muslim reflection, Islam is usually seen as a faith of the sword. For a variety of ideological reasons, Islam has always had and continues to have a very bad press in the West. Political violence, it seems, is a characteristic feature of Muslim activity.

Few ordinary Westerners would be inclined to view Islam as a religion of the pen. And who could blame them? Even a cursory glance at some recent titles and documentaries on the subject would confirm them in their original conviction. Books such as *The Dagger of Islam,*

Sacred Rage, The Holy Killers of Islam, television documentaries such as 'The Sword of Islam', 'The Fire of Islam' – all of this hardly supports any image of Islam as an intellectual religion. Everywhere violent idioms such as 'terror', 'rage', 'dagger', spice the title and trigger off reactions, variously, of withdrawal, anger, fear and contempt from readers located firmly within the Western constituency, in virtue of geography as well as of ideology and prejudice.

In his own way, even a sophisticated scholar such as Cragg merely helps to abet these confused and stereotypical assessments. He continually insinuates that the Prophet overlooked the spiritual axiom that hearts are never won by force. All one can plead in defensive response here is that if the Islamic victory over the pagan Arab conscience had been based on the external persuasions of imposed force, it could scarcely have been so enduring. If one looks objectively at the colossal expansion of the Muslim enterprise well beyond its Arabian confines, it is difficult to credit that the pagan heart, making allowances for some hypocritical, timeserving or otherwise lukewarm allegiances, remained unconquered by the faith. Those of Cragg's priestly forebears who presided over the Inquisition in reconquered Spain would have had little patience with his suggestion that Muslim populations need a state to bolster their faith. And the destruction of the Islamic states by the colonial powers of the last century did not result in a mass crisis of faith; rather, Islam seems to have survived somewhat better under secular administration than has Christianity. It is impossible to remain unimpressed by the heroic quality of Muslim sacrifice in the path of Islam – a feature that remains so distinctive a hallmark of Muslim religious passion even in an allegedly godless twentieth century.

'To study Islam,' writes Cragg, 'both in its history and its theology, is to encounter the most resolute and unperturbed of all faiths in placing trust, and finding pride, in political religion' (*Muhammad and the Christian*, p. 32). In his own context, Cragg does not stop to probe the reason for the trust and the pride. The issues remain. Is the trust well-placed? Is the pride legitimate here? The reason for both is crucial. Political religion here reflects the Islamic conception of *deity*, not simply an arbitrary Muslim conception of *polity*. It is God that we serve; and we serve Him in our political life too. There would be reason for shame, not pride, if the political arm were to be embraced for its own sake rather than for furthering the pious designs of revealed faith.

God also votes for a political group – the party of God (*ḥizb Allāh*). For God is, according to the Muslim scripture, not neutral in the fight between justice and oppression. Nor is this to annex the divine to one's own purely personal cause. The cause of justice is not anyone's private business: it is the public cause *par excellence*.

The virtue of political religion – and it is a virtue at once cardinal in and characteristic of Islam – is its honesty about the periodic need for force in an imperfect constituency. Muslim political involvement, taking its cue from the political activism of the Prophet, is direct and sincere in its mood. And Muslims have always rightly refused to be victimized by arguments employing an alien logic – especially when the premises of such arguments lead to compromises with injustice.

19

There is another positive side to political religion which Cragg is committed to ignoring if not denying. Christianity does not provide a habitat for the flourishing of what the Greeks knew as the 'political virtues'. True, it would be a parody to claim that Christians have no involvement with power: at the very least we are all obliged to have dealings with the worldly powers and principalities of the day. But without full-blooded participation in the political life, how can one develop some of the virtues of civic life? Active citizenship is a precondition of the cultivation of the political virtues. And Islam insists on allowing the sea of faith a specifically political estuary. Furthermore, to reject the political life is effectively to freeze at its source one of the springs of morally excellent behaviour in community. Civil society is the nursery of the political virtues.

'Political' demand enlarges the sphere of 'religious' duty. This is not to say that piety is unattainable unless one lifts one's aspirations beyond the local charities of the self, family and neighbourhood. But it is to say that participation in the political life can be an occasion for developing qualities of character whose value or benefit is by no means limited to the civic life. There are many virtues that are engendered by one's involvement in local, national and even imperial citizenship. Among these is, prominently, the virtue of being vigilant about the rise of militant evil likely to injure the common good. For, naive as it sounds, it is true none the less that if good men leave the civic field free for the miscreants, the miscreants are bound to gain power. For evil to triumph, it is more than sufficient that good men should do nothing to prevent it from doing so.

This is not to deny that such evil may seek the patronage of the religious establishment itself. Where the political virtues may in principle flourish, there too do the political vices build their nest. Corrupt religious personnel may seek personal aggrandizement by exploiting the gullibility of an unalert citizenry. The political life can beget a spirit of impiously calculating realism and an unscrupulous opportunism which make for callousness of heart and kill honour by habituating conscience to devious manipulation and compromise. Such indeed are the risks. Yet the Muslim mind, properly nurtured and humble before God, never loses sight of the ultimate goal. Is it not of the very basis of *islām* that the piety which welcomes power as the effective instrument for the enactment of religious conviction must yet reckon with a higher divine tribunal? And that tribunal deplores the vices that the abuse of power brings in its train. There can be no doubt that political life, even more than the sexual, stands in need of strong internal devices for monitoring its own abuses. Islamic law, which no traditional administration would dare to tamper with, places firm limitations on the ruler's authority. And within the

House of Islam, those who have abused power and perpetrated injustice have periodically been overthrown where
it has been felt (or imagined) that rebellion and revolution
were preferable to the benefits of stability in an otherwise
largely corrupt order. Muslims have never pretended to be
waiting for the process of history to patronize just causes.

The question of the use and abuse of power is, of course,
part of a much larger issue which may briefly be mentioned
before continuing our exploration. Should one completely
forsake a facility for fear of its potential abuse? Cragg
would, in the case of power, proffer an affirmative verdict.
Yet as a general rule, such a stipulation is manifestly
unreasonable. For there are many resources in human life
– the appetite for knowledge and sexuality included –
which are capable both of a right enjoyment and, sadly,
of a wrongful indulgence. The knowledge that provides
refrigerators and medicines also provides bombs and bullets. Likewise with sexuality: the facility that perpetuates
the human heritage, with all the delicious paraphernalia
of tenderness and love, is yet also an arena for private
vulnerability and public exploitation. Should one abjure
the employment of a facility merely for fear of its abuse?
Should one cultivate ignorance because knowledge is liable
to misuse?

We may well wish to leave these larger issues unre-
solved. But it is worth adding that Muslims do not bet on
every horse: if a facility has little or no potential benefit
but could cause much potential or actual harm – think of
alcohol here – then it is indeed to be abjured completely.
But a total veto on power, knowledge or sexuality is
thought not only to be part of an evidently unrealistic ideal
but, more important, it is believed that the proper, morally
constrained, recruitment of these facilities is on balance
likely to produce more good than harm.

20

Judged by modern Christian standards, Muhammad the
politician was bound to be a failure. But Muslims have

wanted to know the exact nature of the Christian reservation here. That Cragg should reject the power dimension does not of course give an exceptional character to his interpretation of Christianity. But his mature indictment of Islam, on broadly Christian principles, is distinctive and worthy of rejoinder.

One of the complicating factors here is the fact that Christianity, unlike Islam, can be divorced from its political heritage. Islamic political institutions are Islamic by definition. In post-Enlightenment Christianity at any rate, the political institutions of Christian nations are not necessarily Christian. In fact, there is now no such thing as Christian politics (in the sense in which there certainly is an Islamic politics). Even so, there is a distinctively Christian perspective on power and polity. And it is a perspective which categorically rejects the style of political religion which Islam adopts.

It may well be reserved for our modern Muslim generation to impart new life to the fast-perishing belief in the ethics of constraint. Most Christian thought on polity and power sadly remains fixated on the pernicious illusion of an ideal world in which the militancy of evil withers away in the face of the accusations of the private conscience – whether ours or theirs. The truth is too obviously the other way: it is the private conscience which is withering away. Evil is in the wrong – but it is strong. And in the real world, to do nothing in the physical field is already to vote for evil.

These are not merely 'academic' thoughts. They have clear implications for political practice. The struggle for social justice in a country such as South Africa is, for example, necessarily long and painful. But it must be a struggle that is free from the wrong kind of inhibition. In such a context of overwhelming injustice, we should jettison certain unrealistic and supposedly Christian principles. 'Turn the other cheek', seen as an untenable principle of social and political morality as opposed to a viable approach to private injury, is a good place to begin. Those who are most eloquent in castigating the sword of retaliation in their official ethics are, paradoxically, best known for their expertise in using it.

At the end of the day, the conclusion must be faced that we cannot keep our hands clean of the political muck. The professed Christian attitude towards power and polity, ever since the compromise with the Emperor Constantine, is the outcome of moral fraud – whether conscious or otherwise. That even a faith originally so vehemently committed, for reasons theological, to stay clear of the political realm should none the less get embroiled in worldly power is a fact that cannot rightly be ignored. And its lessons for the Christian conscience are clear enough. That a creed consciously aiming to remain powerless should none the less find itself so extensively empowered in its subsequent history is a telling commentary on our instinctive need to embrace the political arm. There are here other instructively paradoxical ways in which the ideal of non-violence and powerlessness can be implicated in violent struggle – for example by the way in which it can perversely arouse in powerful establishments an even greater desire for inflicting violence on the powerless. More plausibly, creeds with non-violent commitments have, when eventually empowered, often prostituted power precisely because, unlike the adherents of political religion, their votaries have had no previous or regular doctrinal guidance for regulating belligerent impulses. We need not introduce nuance into these arguable views here. It is enough to note the irony of a civilization in which peace prizes are patronized by gunpowder merchants. Nor, sadly, are all the paradoxes in this area as innocent, let alone as sincere, as this one.

We are, as Greek wisdom teaches, political beings. In Islamic thought too, man is essentially a political being inasmuch as he is God's deputy on earth (Koran 2:30). It is not just that we must have dealings with the political order of our day; that is inevitable. Rather, our pursuit of power is as natural and instinctive as the sex drive. The real question concerns its regulation. For all ideologies survive by courtesy of power. That is why there is a fraud, if a pious one, in the claim that authentically religious ambition can, even in principle let alone in practice, afford to disown 'the things of Caesar'.

21

'This time, either Islam triumphs – or we disappear.' The author of this stark ultimatum, scribbled in a private apartment, is Ayatollah Khomeini, the addressee a fellow revolutionary, the place Tehran just hours before the climax of the Islamic revolution. Triumph or annihilation appear as the only options to the uncompromising writer. Decades of patience and preaching, years of a 'strategic acquiescence with evil' (*taqīya*) are about to end with a mature piety eager to show its true quality. The will to truth, denied an opportunity earlier, owing to fear of violent reprisal, is about to make good its deficiency and hence its vocation.

To refuse to move from the realm of preaching to that of activism is seen as a subtle form of compromise. For militant evil can only be dislodged by the forces of good in an equally militant posture. It is time therefore, the author of the note reasons, to confront the enemy in the final battle – in the sphere of physical power. The pen is mightiest with the sword.

This is certainly a dramatic verdict. But so it should be; for it appropriately underlines the temperament of any proper enquiry into the role of power in human affairs. For such enquiries ought not to be merely professional and relaxed, but rather sincere and urgent. Even academic controversy here should be translatable into practical forms rather than be indulged merely for the love of argument. The debate is about the harsh realities of a fallible political order made fatally dangerous by human avarice and arrogance. In such a setting, Islam has offered us a relevant verdict. Any attempt to ignore or discount it would serve, criminally, to marginalize the things that count – the things of God.

5   The Fellowship of Faith and Force?

'What if you are killed or you die in the cause of God?'
Forgiveness from God and mercy are better than all that men
hoard. (Koran, 3:157)

1

Faith is as faith does; and Muslims always, characteristically, insist on setting the varied tensions and inner stresses
of the individual conscience fairly and squarely within the
social context of allegiance to the community of faith. For
there is no other proper place for the believer seeking to
do God's will. Islam has always imposed an operative veto
on forms of piety divorced from the hurly-burly of life in
all its treacherous detail of fealty, betrayal and the inner
tensions of conscience that are an inevitable part of the
human burden. The biography of the believer may well
typically gravitate towards a crisis where he must make
good his claim that 'there is no power worthy of worship
except God'. Issues of witness and martyrdom, whether in
passive defencelessness or violent struggle, then arise,
taking the final and full measure of one's fidelity to the
religious vocation received, via grace, and finally perfected
– whether through worldly vindication against the multiple
and militant calumnies of evil, or within the justice of the
perfect supernatural nemesis yet to come.

One such biography, setting an example of Muslim passion in the twentieth century, is that of Sayyid Quṭb of the
Egyptian Muslim Brotherhood. The life of this martyr is
instructive in numerous ways – as indicative of scholarly
commitment to the Islamic faith, fearless opposition to
wrong in both social and personal forms, and of a remark-

able capacity to suffer, even in the face of callous witness, for the sake of ultimate convictions.

Born in a small Egyptian village, Quṭb went on to study literature at Cairo University. His search for learning brought him, like some of his richer countrymen, to the United States in the 1940s. After a period of research, he returned to his native land, thoroughly disillusioned with the West and its culture. From the early 1950s onwards, and until his death in 1966, he stood unequivocally for the pristine Islam of the first Muslim community.

It was the Muslim Brotherhood, founded in 1928 by the saintly Ḥasan al-Banna, that totally absorbed Quṭb's political allegiance and gave colour to his ambitions. This was a revivalist movement with a strong emphasis on the virtues of Islam as a unified enterprise of private faith and public ideology. Quṭb was instinctively attracted to an interpretation of Islam that took account of issues of justice and oppression and, more important, provided a workable mechanism for effecting redress and curing social ills. Islam had to be the answer.

After several years of purely verbal, and, generally, fruitless preaching, Quṭb became increasingly convinced that he had to face the entire power structure that resisted Islamic rule – and to do so in the sphere of physical power. He saw that any lack of activism at that crucial hour would be effectively a form of compromise with wrong. Accordingly, in a major act of *imitatio Muhammadi*, he moved to his Medina and continued the campaign.

After the removal of the selfish dictator King Farouk, the military régime of Gamal Abd al-Nasser dominated the scene. But the leaders of the Muslim Brotherhood soon recognized that this new order stood for profane principles; the whole thing was no better than a change of tyrannies. For Nasser's commitment to Egyptian nationalism, and to political effort divorced from all moral scruple, severely and, in the event, permanently alienated the Brothers. As so often happens in Middle Eastern revolutions, the Islamic party and the nationalist faction had united against a common oppressor, in this case King Farouk. But once the common enemy was unseated, unity was at an end. The Nasser régime was perturbed by the presence and disciplined opposition of the Muslim activists who certainly meant business; there was a growing fear of sedition and conspiracy from an alternative power-base. In the eyes of the rulers, there were only two kinds of Muslim Brothers – those who supported the status quo, and those who should be in jail.

Quṭb was put in jail. There he took up his pen again. Like many thinkers before and since in the Islamic world, his authenticity was to be indirectly confirmed by a spell behind bars. And imprisonment has always been a great spur to scholarship and *tadabbur* (reflection). Quṭb worked on his *Fī Ẓilāl al-Qur'ān* (*In the Shade of the Qur'an*), a work of scholarly piety that many regard as rivalling the major traditional works of commentary on the scripture of Islam. It was to be Quṭb's last opportunity to indulge his long if intermittent love affair with Arabic literature and his final chance to savour the most moving beauty of 'this amazing book', as he fondly calls his scripture.

Upon his release in 1964, Quṭb did not relax his Islamic conscience. His work as a social reformer was cut out for him. God had sent down 'the Book and the balance in order that men may do justice' – to rise up to justice. Quṭb had been preparing himself for the final act of piety. He published his stirring work of prose entitled *Milestones on the Path*. It provoked the corrupt rulers; the work proved to be a preface to his martyrdom.

When tried in 1965 for plotting against the Egyptian régime, Quṭb, with a bravery reminiscent of Sir Thomas More, not only conceded the accusation but expatiated on it. He argued that defiance of evil structures was an Islamic duty, not some private option of the pious will. And loyalty to God and the community of Islam supersedes a profane fealty to the Egyptian motherland: *Allāhu akbar* ('God is greater'). Quṭb was merely, in his own opinion, calling evil by its name and thereby endangering his own life. But he saw it as the only way to obey the divine imperative. No

doubt, he would have claimed God Himself for his tutor;
Sūra 4, v. 135:

O you who believe! Be resolute in the doing of justice, as
witnesses to God, even though it be against your own selves,
your parents, or your kith and kin, whether it concern men
rich or poor, for God is nearer to both. Do not follow your
own whims lest you swerve. And if you do distort justice or
decline to do it, truly, God is well-acquainted with all that
you do.

Quṭb was found guilty of treason and executed in 1966.
His complete trust in God and patient endurance (*ṣabr*) in
the hour of trial were destined to become exemplary for
the other Brothers and, as news seeped outside Egypt, for
the larger Muslim community outside Arab confines. It is
not for us to speculate here about what the rare combi-
nation of moral excellence and intellectual genius in Quṭb's
personality might have added to the world's stock of piety
had his life not been terminated by a corrupt generation.

Sayyid Quṭb is by no means the only martyr for the
cause of Islam in this century. But he is certainly among
the greatest. For the quality of his conviction alone would
put him in that category. Once he had put his bet on Islam,
he relied entirely on the all-sufficient grace of God. There
were many occasions to cultivate *ṣabr*, that most koranic
of the virtues. Quṭb was admired by many lesser Brothers
for the dignity and trust with which he endured moments
of eclipse. As would be expected with an authentically
Muslim temper, one looks in vain even for a trace of the
tragic impulse. (Cragg, in his *The Pen and the Faith*, looks,
fails to find it, and records it as a deficiency in the martyr.)
All vicissitude is from God – to be borne with patience
and gratitude. 'Yes to life' remains the attitude even in the
harsh environment of prison, with all its severe deprivations and consequent paucity of occasion for expressing
the will to gratitude. Shot through the entire fabric of
Quṭb's patience is the spirit of the sacred volume when it
sets down complete indifference to profane and ignorant

verdicts as the final proof of the strength of the man of God.

2

. . . Islam is worship, leadership, religion, state, spirituality, patience, prayer, *jihād*, obedience, judgement, the Book, and the sword.

The Book and the sword! A striking juxtaposition indeed; but by no means an un-Islamic one. The author of the quoted creed was not Sayyid Quṭb. The words were in fact penned by his tutor, Ḥasan-al-Banna – also martyred – founder of the Muslim Brotherhood, whose preaching and activism alike are among the most rigorous in twentieth-century Islam.

Prayer and the sword – to select another possible conjunction from the list – would also, to a modern Christian, seem discrepant allies. But al-Banna, like the many men and women he taught, always saw the two as aspects of a single, authentically koranic piety. In doing so, they have copied the style of the Prophet's own unified militancy: prayer and the pen in the private sector of piety need to be supplemented, where necessary, with the sanctions of power and polity in the public domain. The power dimension was seen, no doubt rightly, as instinctively central to a truly comprehensive religious ideal. Whether it was violence inflicted or endured – in the way of God – it was inescapable. The Kingdom of God could not be some apolitical fantasy of the purely 'religious' imagination.

'The Book and the sword', reads the clause. It has a frightening quality of inevitable conflict about it. The divine imperative is unavoidably caught up in worldly opposition and violent confrontation as the profane establishment seeks to thwart it. It is unfortunate that things have to be this way. But there we have it. The truly religious mind, that of Quṭb, for instance, willingly sacrifices itself to absolute revealed authority. In some moods one may feel moved to question or regret what such authority has demanded. The standards certainly seem too high. (Quṭb's family members were tortured; and *Allāhu akbar* is certainly an imperative easier said than obeyed.) In the event, both Quṭb and al-Banna were martyred by establishments which feared the sincerity of their opponents' militancies.

The quality and context of Quṭb's martyrdom is significant, especially as it naturally involves issues, raised by Christian critics, about the Muslim style (or styles) of sacrifice in the service of God. Quṭb's witness was within a pattern of worldly defeat, without the 'signal triumph' that crowned the Prophet's political endeavours.

In his *Social Justice in Islam*, Quṭb stressed the value of preaching, education, and 'the pen'. Those were, in a sense, early days. The conviction rapidly grew in Quṭb's mind that he would need to sacrifice himself for the renewal of the Islamic religion. He must surely have realized, rightly, that a faith can survive indefinitely without thinkers but not without martyrs. In any case, the Koran constantly demanded dying and, if necessary, killing as part of a religious obligation due to God. Accordingly, Quṭb hints at his own coming martyrdom in the final chapter of *Milestones on the Path*.

The insinuation comes in what is an otherwise unaccountably melancholy commentary on the koranic chapter *al-Burūj*. Quṭb reflects reverently on the fate of the ancient 'martyrs of the pit' who were burnt to death because they stood their ground as monotheistic believers. Quṭb notes that, oddly, the Koran here does not make any comment about retribution; evil seems to triumph in this world. Presumably the victory of the righteous is reserved for another realm.

It is one of Quṭb's signal achievements to have reintroduced the centrality of martyrdom back into mainstream Sunnī Islam. Moreover, it was a martyrdom incurred as persecution and in the face of callous witness, as opposed to a death incurred during violent conflict in the pursuit of empire and worldly success. Shī'ite tradition had always had a cult of martyrdom, but Sunnī Islam, with its successes and political confidence, had not attached much importance to it lately. Quṭb brought it back into mainstream Islam as a cardinal obligation, not merely as some act of supererogation.

3

'Those who do not judge in accordance with what God has revealed,' warns *Sūra al-Māʿida* (v. 44) 'are surely evildoers.' In its implications, *de facto* Muslim rulers are within the scope of this accusation. Quṭb, in line with authentically koranic sentiments, urged violent revolt and resistance to a régime he judged unworthy of Muslim allegiance. In his discussion of the career of Quṭb, Cragg makes several highly questionable claims of which one deserves careful examination. The issue centres around the notion of the possibility of a post-koranic age of ignorance in which, notwithstanding the presence of Islam in the world, many so-called Muslims are lured, mainly through Western influences, back into the 'days of ignorance' (*jāhilīya*) as these obtained in Arabia before the advent of Islam.

Cragg claims to be puzzled by the devout Muslim's eagerness to maintain that the presence of un-Islamic rulers is evidence that idolatry still flourishes even within the citadel of official Islam – even after fourteen centuries of the faith (*The Pen and the Faith*, pp. 60ff.). But surely these are the facts. Should one call idolatry by any other name? And there is little ground for Christian triumphalism here. For the very same idolatry persists despite two thousand years of Christianity – and increasingly flourishes in the very heart of modern Christendom. Christians do not see the law as sufficient for the removal of perversity. Fair enough; but Christianity is in no better shape when it comes to eliminating idolatry. The dispute between Islam and Christianity is not solely over plumbing the precise depth of sinfulness. There are no prizes, least of all in this century, for fearing that sinfulness is inveterate. The matter that counts is to do with its effective removal from the human heart. And no honest observer of the Muslim world today can fail to notice and register, if not regret, the blights of 'Westoxication' (in Jalāl Āl-e Aḥmad's phrase) and idolatry among the ruling sections of the peoples of Islam. Quṭb identified it, called it by its name, and opposed it. Islam demands nothing less of any of its adherents.

In his discussion of Quṭb's career, Cragg urges predictably that one needs to ask who the real Muslims are – Quṭb and the Brothers or their opponents? Fair enough; but Cragg wrongly implies that the dispute here is intractable. Islam is a religion conclusively and fully defined by the scripture which historically inspired the man who established it. In the dispute between Quṭb and his enemies, no Muslim has a choice about the matter. Copies of the Koran are to hand; and claims about latitude of interpretation, especially when made by outsiders, are liable to exaggeration. One might say, admittedly rather provocatively, that given interpretations of Islam are either one hundred per cent right or wholly wrong. Islam lends itself to such conclusive judgements, given its own clarity of vision and married as it is to an unflinching repudiation of double standards. Quṭb's interpretation of Islam is wholly correct. Cragg himself explicitly states that Quṭb's attitudes are authentically koranic (*The Pen and the Faith*, p. 62) and his militancy is similar to the Prophet's own (*ibid.*, p. 54). If so, doesn't Quṭb qualify as a true Muslim? And if that be granted, how can those who wished to destroy him, who made no secret of their indifference to the basic ethical and devotional obligations of the faith, be better Muslims?

For the outsider, like Cragg, this still leaves on one's hands the major problem of who is right. But such a question is not open for those who embrace Islam. For the believer, if a position is authentically Islamic, it has to be right. And the matter is resolved. In such a context appeals to the complexity of traditions are unacceptably contrived. The fact that there are indeed matters of detail concerning which Muslims differ among themselves does not imply that there are radical divisions of opinion over matters of fundamental self-definition. Cragg's discussion is instructive. For it is one of the many examples of the way in which otherwise intelligent enquiry can deteriorate into polemical insinuation once faced with genuinely Islamic tempers of mind and devotion.

There is one further and final issue here. 'If there were a God, I'd jail him along with you,' said Nasser in an evil taunt to the imprisoned Qutb. Nasser here speaks eloquently on behalf of many in the Islamic world – fellow conspirators with the West in their opposition to Muslim political ambition in their own territories.

The contemporary Muslim conscience, justly provoked, should no longer entrust the current state of injustice to patience, prayer and the unpredictable future. In Sayyid Qutb and kindred patterns of sincere militancy, all Muslims have found necessarily inspiring and trustworthy advocates.

Conclusions: The Final Imperative

the truth remains unruined
god's reply to oppression never changes

Shabbir Banoobhai

1

Buddhism has been described as the 'Christianity of the East'. If we leave aside the quibble that there is strictly speaking, in terms of origins, no Christianity of the West for the implied contrast to be meaningful, the description is not an unfair one. For there is a recognition here that there are religious religions and political religions. Modern Christianity and Buddhism are essentially religions of private salvation calling for humble postures of powerlessness within and against worldly structures. Islam, by contrast, is a faith which incorporates morally constrained political action. The Prophet certainly inculcated in his followers a very firm sense of the colossal social responsibility that genuine – the adjective is here necessary – religion incurs: fidelity to Islam can entail political activism here and now. God too votes for a political party; and every human religious solidarity is naturally eager to annex Him.

It has taken Marxism to teach Christians that private piety is almost futile in a world of large-scale political failure. But Marxists can claim no such didactic favour with respect to Muslims. Far from dulling men's political consciousness, Islam has often agitated the masses, demanding revolt and enjoining sacrifice in the context of holy struggle (*jihād*) against militant forms of evil. Certainly, there is something amiss about the familiar socialist criticism, often levelled indifferently at all theists, that the religious promise of heavenly compensation for earthly wretchedness has effectively imposed on human society a passivity even in the face of gross injustice. This reservation is almost entirely nourished on experiences that have transpired in Western Christian lands. Passivity is foreign to the very instincts of Islam – a religion of action. Whatever may be said of the political vigour of contemporary Jewish and Christian dispensations, Muhammad's political religion continues to topple the dynasties. In the field of political militancy, 'applied Islam' is undeniably the star performer. Muslims justifiably boast about its unique amalgam of irreducible religious and political enthusiasms inspiring as it consequently does the highest rate of martyrdom of any living faith. A central issue in theistic religion is: how may one render God's truth attractive, and victorious? By somehow adding glamour even to the apparently unspectacular cause of righteousness, Islam solves the issue decisively.

Islam and its spokesmen continually remind believers of their social and political obligations. Among these is the obligation to ensure that the faith is not compromised or annexed. Islam cannot be a nationalized industry. Many princes and kings have tried to domesticate it but none has wholly succeeded. No ruler (with the grim exception of Enver Hoxha the late Albanian Communist leader) has yet dared to forbid the Friday assembly – a potentially political association that threatens corrupt rulers. There are preachers, especially in countries such as Egypt, who take their belongings with them on Fridays knowing that their uncompromising sermons will induce the corrupt powers to arrest them at the end of the service. And who would dare openly to oppose a religion that produces men of such character?

Muslims are a people who know themselves – know themselves to be a power to be reckoned with. They take their cue from the sacred volume which describes them as a just and balanced community forbidding what is wrong, enjoining what is right, who walk on the middle path, the straight road.

I have argued in this book that the morally constrained

employment of power should be seen as an intrinsic demand of an all-encompassing Islamic faith, not as a lapse from moral integrity necessitated by recalcitrant circumstance. The Prophet saw no good reason why a resourceful sovereignty should be denied the last word in the world merely on account of certain baseless qualms about the recruitment of force. As long as methods of constraint were legitimately and properly applied, the use of political power was not only not wrong, it was positively right. Muslims, unlike their detractors, have never pretended to be waiting for history to patronize good causes.

At root, the involvement with power is, in both the Islamic and the Marxist visions, the outcome of the conviction that human suffering, to the extent that it is not inevitable, remains essentially an exclusively political phenomenon. Islam, like Marxism, recognizes the possibility of a prosperous and just social order here on earth. Christianity, to take another vision, sees – or rather should in principle see – the radical sinfulness of human nature as imposing an operative embargo on the possibility of social justice on this side of the grave. Man's fallen state entails a permanent social disability that no political order could remove. Christianity, like Buddhism, views much of human suffering as an apolitical feature of our plight, transcending as it does purely political resolution. Islam and Marxism, by contrast, are characterized by an integral concern with the conscientious use of power in the service of social change that, in turn, serves to eliminate avoidable varieties of our distress and misery.

2

All learned authorities are unanimous that the first koranic sequence (Koran 96:1–5) had ordered the Prophet to 'recite' certain words – an act from which the sacred volume derives its title. 'Recite in the name of thy Lord, Who teaches man, by the pen, that which he knew not.' The emphasis here is straightforwardly educational. Some time later, after a painfully barren hiatus familiar to prophets and mystics, the voice from Heaven ordered Muhammad to warn his compatriots about Allah's conclusive, if deferred, judgement against a rejecting generation (Koran 74:1ff.). The question of the relationship between religious truth and the rôle of (secular) power in defending, confirming or establishing it was at the top of the agenda.

There is no intractable dispute among students of the Koran concerning the date of revelation of the first passage that sanctioned militant struggle. The details in any case form part of a debate that amuses experts. We have simply noted the scripture's overall attitude towards the use and abuse of force in social conflict. A religious enterprise sincerely concerned to implement its message must, if it is to make good its sincerity and intention, not only will the end but also the appropriate means. The rest of the Islamic tale here is familiar. It has fallen to the lot of the Muslim apologists to justify the use of force in the service of extending the witness to the dominion of Allah – far beyond the confines of the *Jazīrat al-'Arab* (the Arabian peninsula). The related problem of transforming physical power into legitimate social authority is a perennial one in Islamic political philosophy – an anxiety Muslim reflection shares with political philosophy of every ideological origin and complexion.

We have examined the Christian charge. The Caesar in Muhammad's nature, it is said, took control at Medina. It was a betrayal of the prophetic vocation in the dark hour of worldly power. The alternative patterns are a Jesus in the enduring dignity of meek patience, a Jeremiah who cried unto death in the wilderness, and indeed Muhammad himself in the Meccan years of travail and defeat. Nor were the Arabian iconoclast's motives for desiring success necessarily unworthy ones: he wanted God's purpose to have the upper hand, remain in the field despite human arrogance and perversity. How noble a purpose! But, sadly, the accusation concludes, he misunderstood the nature of victory in matters of the spirit: God's aims are sometimes vindicated even in, indeed especially in, the pattern of worldly failure. To the modern Christian, the

Koran's 'clear victory' (Koran 48:1) for Muhammadan militancy is a failure in the eyes of the highest arbiter of destiny.

Kenneth Cragg has expatiated on the Muslim failure to grasp the logic of divine triumph. The issue has always been close to the hearts of Muslims and Christians. And it is tempting to close the case decisively. We have tried to keep it open. It will be for dogmatists in both camps to close what is best kept open – open to challenge and reverent critique. And to God belongs the conclusive case in the affair.

The Christian view of the rôle of power is, given the assumptions that nourish it, perfectly intelligible, perhaps even justified. Certainly, it is unsurprising once we note that Jesus, unlike Moses before him and Muhammad after him, and despite the fragility of our historical picture of his life, appears never to have founded a polity. It is true that there is some rather equivocal support – in a speech probably attributed to him by the clergy at a later stage – for the establishment of a Church. But the Church, as *corpus Christi*, is nowadays seen as an institution proclaiming the power of the spirit, so to speak, rather than as laying the foundations of a socio-political order in the standard sense. The idea of such an order has often been suspect in Christianity. It is quite likely that Jesus himself, given the significance of eschatological expectations and the perception of the imminence of divine judgement within the outlook of first-century Palestinian Judaism, saw the suggestion of an established political state as a superfluity. Alternatively, as many academics have suggested, it may be that Christianity originated as an esoteric, mystical brotherhood which was never intended to be wrenched from the Law, being vouchsafed 'only to the lost sheep of the Children of Israel'. But at any rate, much subsequent Christian thought has characteristically been of the opinion that, since the integrity of human nature was destroyed by original sin, men are incapable of attaining a prosperous and just order here on earth. Power cannot remove or mitigate the disability entailed by radical sin: as long as men are corrupt at heart, they cannot establish a fully just society. Unsurprisingly, then, Christians have discerned a religious sanction for entertaining a moral suspicion about the use of worldly power in the service of socio-political ends.

The Islamic story is a different one, the differences rooted in opposed theological preconceptions about the Deity and human nature. Men and women are religiously obliged to establish the Kingdom of God on earth – a prosperous social order in which citizens adhere to a sacred Law. Since man is not inherently corrupt or fallen, he has the capacity to recruit power in the service of faithful ends. Islam in principle recognizes no distinction between the religious and the secular spheres of life; all is, from 'the womb to the tomb' in Arthur Miller's phrase, and indeed beyond, placed under a righteous sovereignty. The political is no exception. Every resource and facility is to be harnessed in the service of a comprehensive Lordship.

Frithjof Schuon puts the contrast this way:

A very important aspect of Christian morality, not so much its social as its intrinsic morality, is its refusal to exact justice: this attitude presupposes our consciousness of immanent justice on the one hand and of our own quasi-congenital injustice on the other, natural egoism and the danger of pride being traces of the Fall . . .

On the question of justice, as on that of pleasure, Islam maintains a balanced and non-contrasting attitude: while integrating into its perspective the point of view of Christ, it also takes into account the rights of nature; it takes into account the fact that not only is every natural right in itself harmless to the soul, but that it also comprises a possibility of virtue and mystical alchemy, failing which, precisely, it would not be natural. This means that the Moslem on the one hand draws the sword 'for God' and 'by God' and, on the other, draws it without forgetting to be generous, wherever generosity can and should be shown; this is, at least in principle, the perspective of Islam, to be applied by every Moslem who is scrupulously faithful to the Sunna [The prophetic exemplar].

(*Christianity/Islam. Essays in Esoteric Ecumenicism.*
Bloomington: World Wisdom Books, 1985, pp. 138–9)

Power can be, indeed, often is, misused. We know this because there is a morality here. All is certainly not fair in war; and it is for romantic pundits to legislate about love. The mere fact, however, that power is liable – is even particularly liable – to misuse is neither here nor there. For every facility, especially every facility of worth, necessarily conceals a potential for misuse. Is the fact that, say, knowledge can be misused, an argument then in favour of cultivating ignorance? Knowledge can indeed occasionally lead one astray; but ignorance never fails to achieve that end. Admittedly, power, like knowledge, can be used for good or ill; and powerful individuals are as capable of virtue as of vice. It is, however, morally truistic to hold that power should be used properly; but it is morally absurd to say that power should never be recruited even in the service of the just cause. The use of force is often enough caused by the lust for domination and personal gain. But it is an unempirical view of history and human nature which pontificates that the employment of force can never rightly be instigated by a search for justice, equality, truth, and social compassion in an imperfect order, often enough in rebellion against its own ultimate interests.

To embrace, if reluctantly, the political arm in a world where the intransigence of social conflict impresses every perceptive student is not to make an idol of it. God forbid. Power is, in the Islamic outlook, not an end. The end is peace; and the mandate for peace is easily and plentifully found in a Koran that contains, to the surprise of Christian detractors, at least as much support for it as any other sacred scripture. But Islam, with its single standards of justice, has always – and rightly – rejected peace where such a circumstance was effectively contaminated by injustice. Peace without justice cannot endure; peace with justice must necessarily abide.

That Christians should, in the area of toleration and reconciliation, cast the first stone is a matter for some amazement. Christianity's own moral record in such matters as pluralism, toleration and coercion, judged by modern, internal Christian standards, is, as some churchmen now concede, utterly deplorable. For though the Christian community has never defended intolerance as an ideal, it would be difficult to find many among its members in the past who have avoided intolerance in practice. Islam, however, judged by standards intrinsic to the faith, has always had a strikingly good record. Indeed, in general, Islam's record is, even when judged by exterior, allegedly higher Christian standards, honourably distinguished by its relative tolerance of alien conviction.

3

With God as teacher and man as a promising, if at times wayward, student, Islam recognizes no mundane category or facility higher than the prophethood (*nubuwwa*) that institutes law and guidance. If we put the matter this way, we can immediately broach a discussion of the central dispute between Christians and Muslims. Does law, along with the auxiliary mechanism of retribution, achieve its own purpose – namely, to get us to achieve our destiny as virtuous agents? Does divine legislation fulfil the divine intention that inspired it? Or do we need something more than the institution of prophethood for the tuition of mankind? And could that higher institution be 'sonship', understood not as some crudely physical relationship but rather as the exemplification of a divine relationship to man – a relationship characterized by initiatives of suffering love and grace? Do we need a God who comes rather than brings, who gives himself to us in unconditional love? Doesn't our condition instinctively crave dimensions of grace and love that a resourceful moral sovereignty is well able to supply?

The Koran sees man as a promising if occasionally disobedient student. He can learn – through repeated exhortation and devout attention to excellent example. But he can also fail – and fail miserably. This double potential – never far from a reverently alert readership engaged with the Koran – is, one might say, in Pascalian idiom, the basis for the union of the grandeur and triumph (*falāḥ*) of the creature with the undoubted historical evidences of misery and radical loss (*khusr*).

Islam and Christianity adopt different positions within their theologies in part because of different positions in their anthropologies. The Christian observation here is that, in view of man's perversity, Islam overestimates the educative influence of religious institutions. Evil is inveterate, not merely a film on the surface of personality. Its deepest reaches are in the heart, and cannot be removed merely by external action or profession. Islam, it is alleged, for all its repeated condemnation of idolatry and man's hard-heartedness, fails to recognize the sheer depth of the perversity that flouts the Law. There can be no evil more inveterate than the perversity that fathers it.

Yet Christianity is, I would argue, in no better shape *vis-à-vis* human recalcitrance than Islam or Judaism. For men are as free to reject the grace of Christ as of Allah or Yahweh. The perversity of man is an irreducible feature of his constitution. Nothing, except God's grace, can cure it conclusively; there are no saving actions that can necessarily save sinners from their own perversity.

The whole logic of prophecy, argues Cragg, demands the saving actions of Christ. Christianity is the natural terminus of Islam. For 'sonship' is the successor institution to prophethood; it is a natural step. Islam, contends Cragg, terminates the divine engagement with man at the level, jejune and bare, of mere law and prophethood. In doing so, it wrongly, and arbitrarily, arrests the movement of divine grace and love into a created order existing precisely because of earlier divine initiatives embodied in law and prophethood.

These are intelligent and deeply felt criticisms of the Islamic religious imagination. Yet the problem here, of course, is that the step Cragg describes as natural is, in fact, not even intelligible. It is actually not a step that a person – including God – can take. Cragg seems unalert to the problem of the *coherence* of the Incarnation and the intelligibility of the related doctrines of the Trinity and Sonship. He writes exclusively of the Incarnation as supplying a richer moral potential; and he argues in detail that Muslims misunderstand the Christian dimension of a suffering divine love when they reject it as an offence to the dignity of God. But granted, for the sake of a case, that the Incarnation has powerful ethical significances absent from the Judaeo-Islamic theological matrix, the question remains whether or not it is coherent. Suspending, for the sake of argument, the Muslim perspectives that see the Incarnation as blasphemous, the question of its coherence must stay. Only after we have established the coherence of the Incarnation can we be in a position to assess its moral potential. It is a further, and necessarily subsequent, issue whether or not such a gesture, meaningfully attained, could ease the normal human travail in fulfilling sacred obligation or drastically cure the perversity of militant evil. But the prior conceptual question must head the agenda. Cragg fails to identify this issue, let alone address it.

That God is supremely great or greater (*akbar*) is certainly a conviction common to all the theisms of Hebrew lineage. The issue that divides them, particularly Christianity and Islam, is precisely *how*, in what way, this divine supremacy is to be understood and interpreted. What makes God greater? (This sounds like a child's deceptively easy question; yet it raises the deepest issues.) Cragg argues, as we saw earlier, that Islam misunderstands the greatness of the divine when it deflects the issue of human perversity into the political dimension, where rejection is subdued rather than redeemed. We need to return briefly now to the questions raised in earlier chapters and examine them from another, more metaphysical, angle. Cragg contends (*Muhammad and the Christian*, p. 128) that Muhammad's recruitment of the political wing was a natural corollary of his belief that prophethood more or less exhausts the resources of a divine sovereignty dealing with a sinful order under sacred tuition. God has warned through His spokesmen; men disregard and ignore. They need to be humbled. But humbled in what way? Cragg's opinion is that once the educative dimension fails to cure perversity – once the pen runs out of ink – the sovereignty that

104

recognizes no further dimensions, has no richer resources, is bound to opt for a coercive technique to get the miscreants in line. For God must succeed; and yet God's party – *hizb Allāh* in koranic terminology – has run out of the only arsenal men of God should use. But if they resort to forceful sanction, then the message is not merely taught but enforced. The sword then becomes mightier than the pen – and all the more mighty for being the only weapon that remains. In that sense, God and His spokesmen do indeed have the last word.

The God of Christian faith, however, argues Cragg, is above this kind of greatness. For when His message fails to educate, His grace and long-suffering are there to pre-empt any premature punitive options. Granted, then, that men have failed the examination, refused to learn the lesson, the properly divine way to redeem this failure is through a yet greater initiative of love and grace – a love that suffers, suffers unjustly, in order to redeem the unjust. It is only human, all too human, to resort to the facility of worldly power in the face of spiritual failure. Divine ends require divine means; and God's spokesman must represent God's way of dealing with mankind. For the weapons and techniques of Muhammad's ministry are to be carried backwards into the character of his God. Islam's central religious confidence, expressed in the slogan *Allāhu akbar*, is denied internally by the Muslim refusal to allow God to be 'greater' than merely the omnipotent Lord who dispatches prophetic instruction manuals for mankind and punishes failure to learn. Why shouldn't so great and resourceful a sovereignty take more radical measures in the larger attempt to frustrate the will to impiety? Why shouldn't it seek to 'redeem' and rehabilitate the evil that it fails to cauterize through mere education? Only a God who can accomplish this would be worthy of worship, would be *akbar*. For only such a God *ought* to have the last word.

Let me begin by signalling agreement on a crucial point. Cragg is right in emphasizing that mere exhortation, no matter how multiple and vehement, condemnations of perversity, threats of punishment, and edificatory speeches do not suffice. Men continue to flout them all. Excellent examples won't do either: the villain and miscreant couldn't care less about the exemplary goodness of the saint or martyr. In the face of enforced religion, the will to perversity simply withdraws deeper into the privacy of the heart; rituals like prayer cannot eliminate hypocrisy. And even collective piety, impressive on account of numbers and ostentatious passions, need not be genuine after the strange thrill of the public gaze is no longer present. And piety when achieved also carries, as the study of hagiography shows, its own temptations and trials. For with that kind of moral excellence belong insidious inner tendencies to self-righteousness and, with a further twist of the spiral, a new, deeper kind of hubris, this time under the aegis of an apparent sanctity.

The perversity of mankind and the disturbing scale of rejection are both facts of religious history. The question is whether or not we can cure this perversity by any mechanism other than preaching and the Law. I think it is incoherent to look for an external rescue from the plight created by human recalcitrance to divine law. To be sure, there is here something of a rut. God warns; men disregard; God punishes and destroys. But there we have it. Such is the ultimate style of the divine art. For man, created free, has an inner, regrettably often dominant, tendency to wrongdoing. Nothing can cure it in most of us (although God mysteriously cured it, by fiat, in the case of the prophets, and reduced it drastically for the saints). The greatness of God consists in doing what is possible. The gesture in the Incarnation is, it seems to me, metaphysically incoherent, though we can well understand the moral stresses that may desire it. It is clearly a burden for the Christian intellect to demonstrate the coherence of this move.

Leaving aside issues of coherence, my own view is that the gesture of humility implicit in the Incarnation is actually of no relevance to the problem of human recalcitrance to the Law of God. For one thing, the setting of excellent examples, whether human or divine, does not radically ease the individual's moral strife. For another, we may reasonably object that obeying the Law is easy enough – for God. It is not enough to retort that Christ was both man and God. For we are simply, plainly, men. We need an uncomplicatedly human exemplar – though, unfortunately, even this may not curb our will to sin. The perversity of man is a fact with which we should simply reckon and then accept. There's no way out of this rut. In one sense, human perversity is often bound to have the last word.

To recognize human recalcitrance is not to deny the urgency of the divine demand upon the human constituency. The religious law is, I would argue, an integral part of the theistic ordinance, of the divine dispensation for a created order. For although God is a kind teacher, He wants the lesson learnt. The face of obligation may justifiably be stern as long as it is not hostile in its final intention. Bondage in matters moral is discriminated from moral freedom not on account of the absence or presence of external restraints – in any case inevitable in our condition – but by a liberating awareness of the origin and nature of limitations and the moral worth of the end they are intended to serve.

The God of Islam, then, is an educator. But it is not as though He knows, like a strict parent, only the word – rather than the blow – of authority and command. Discipline can bring intemperate demands and chastisement; yet a foolish lenience is equally wrong. God supplements education with His grace. The view that God will show mercy to us sinners should not become a refuge for irresponsibility nor yet a ready pretext for neglecting His law. Admittedly, disbelief in the divine mercy is a piece of cardinal infidelity in Islam, for, as the Prophet taught, 'God is more merciful towards His servants than is a mother towards her child.' But once the season of education is over, God wants the lesson learnt. The Lord of Muhammad is compassionate yet vigilant, watching over His servants from the watchtower (*mirsad*).

God, in the Islamic conception, is neither a tragedian nor a sentimentalist. From cover to cover of the Koran, one discerns a total understanding, without illusions, of human nature as it is and of the related need for the firm yoke of the Law. For men do not easily change for the better. The aim of revelation, however, is not to impose, from the outside, unrecognizable duties, but rather to extract from within man an awareness of duties implicitly recognized to be binding. It is in this context that the scripture calls upon its readers time and again to think reverently, to bring their eyes close to the texture of their mortality.

The task of educating man would be a forlorn hope if the material with which the prophet works were unpromising. Scripture appeals to our higher nature, which already acknowledges our duties – and acknowledges all the more for failing to fulfil. It is essential, if a religious ideal is to be viable, that it embodies, albeit in fairer form and considered proportion, the very obligations which men are already to some degree able to fulfil. Effective ideals are a picture of valid human hopes and potentials – not an embarrassing reminder of what is impossible.

But aren't the prophetic injunctions, in some sense, radically new and demanding? Or else why must the divine spokesman, as so often happens, cry in the wilderness to an unheeding multitude? Admittedly, there will be rejection and conscious opposition to the moral ideals of our higher nature. The scriptural claim is that the voice of the warning prophet finds its way into the conscience of those inclined to submission (*islām*). For the ideals that make men authentically human echo the very ideals their higher nature instinctively craves – and according to traditional Muslim confidence, scripture supplies both.

4

Jesus, the pale Galilean, our brother, was not pale in ideal and commitment, whatever racist pundits may say of his complexion. His ideals of submission and righteousness in a world made precarious by human pride and perversity were intellectual as opposed to primitive, innocent as opposed to cynical – all with an intelligent earnestness at their core. Jesus had reached a point in his ministry where he could rightly press a mysterious Providence for an answer to the related riddles of rejection, the intransigence of social conflict, the power and perversity of evil in an essentially righteous order. The Christian apologist claims that in the Christ of God, we have the whole truth. Unsympathetic theists might retort that Jesus never grew old enough in this sordid world to find the answer. If we leave that question to the dogmatists and experts in both camps, we are still required to take a stance on the issue of the relationship between secular power and revealed truth. Islam offers one elaborate verdict whose details have interested us both as a commentary on the nature and reputation of God, as well as on the urgency of political struggle in a human constituency no less imperfect today than on the day our history began.

Islam is, in the best sense of the term, a virginal religion that sets great store by chastity in matters of dogma and morality, spurning the overtures of any devious, duplicitous or otherwise seductive suitors. The faith of the Arabian messenger is a pre-Enlightenment consciousness of the world. More precisely, it belongs to the purer half of our history when theism endorsed single standards of justice and when compromise, where it occurred, was intelligent and restricted to trivial matters.

History gives us no example of a more honest statesman than Muhammad, this prophet-politician from Mecca. His frankness about the need for power is interpreted by critics as a lust for domination at worst and a misplaced fanaticism on behalf of God at best. The truth lies in neither verdict – assuming, of course, that truth is what we seek and, in the case of believers, by the grace of God find.

Islam, in a manner unique to its religious genius, builds the motive for political action, individually and collectively, into the very fabric of its central dogma of the immense ruling reality of God as King. Unsurprisingly, few wise rulers would claim that their own, all too human, governments fully implement a revealed Islam. For God as King naturally dislikes other pretenders to the throne – unless they know their proper place. The Koran radiates an irreducibly consequential political vocabulary of condemnation – a vocabulary immediately invoked when professed ideal and reality become unduly detached. No régime claiming Islamic status could ignore the inveterate and potent influence of koranic dicta on the minds and consciences of the ruled Muslims. Thus, no government is likely to succeed in harnessing Islam fully to its own secular use. Christians have, in the post-Enlightenment world, learnt to live with secular national sovereignties that regularly manipulate the Christian sub-cultures, exploiting them for secular ends. Anglican Christianity, at any rate, is a 'nationalized industry' in the United Kingdom. Muslims, however, reject the view that when the instruments of social justice are distributed, Caesar should get the things that matter while God and His spokesmen get the leftovers. Consequently, all alliances with Islam have to be partly on Islamic terms. Recognizing the dangers of such a religion, all Arab governments have tried to contain its massive moral energy. In practice, all have outlawed Islam as a political force in their territories. Such 'moderate' governments headed by pliant 'Muslim' leaders are essentially neocolonial sovereignties co-operating closely with Western conspirators – secular and Christian – who also view Islam as a false faith with a real potential to endanger the West's political and economic interests.

Islam, however, remains on the Middle Eastern landscape as proudly and as naturally as any natural feature. What ensures its future is a feature internal to its nature. An authentic faith, seeking to perpetuate the heritage of the good, must trade on a fund of fierce anger at the sight of the callous, the graceless, the life-denying, the unjust, the sordid, the impure, the 'inhuman' in the fullest sense of that rich word. Such a temper of constructive yet militant wrath is vital to any ideology that seeks security, an audience, and the triumph of truth in a world of sophisticated impiety, irreligious confidences, deep indifferences and secular preoccupations. For how else are humble men of faith to apprise worldly complacency, with all its powers and principalities, that there are forces greater than the purely human? Western Christianity, fixated on love, has lost all appreciation of the balancing religious function of fear, an emotion without which one cannot even effect personal rectitude, let alone social righteousness.

5

There is a saying of the Prophet, no doubt an intriguing one for modern Christians, which instructs us: 'Do not quest for authority, for if you do so, you will be destroyed by it; whereas if you are given it without asking, you will be given to succeed.'

Muslim history is a tale of dynasties rather than revolutions. While monarchy is by no means the only legitimate form of Islamic government, it has been advocated by those who take the above counsel seriously. For a king does not seek power: he receives it, together with a sense of the honour and responsibility of his line. But the Muslim tradition, expressed most famously here by Ibn Khaldun, also acknowledges that dynasties become decayed and corrupt, and that it is the responsibility of the larger Muslim community to urge the king to reform. If he cannot, they must disobey and depose him.

It is the real threat of such a coup that keeps kings, caliphs and sultans in line. They may be corrupt privately – that is their own business. But when their corruption threatens to corrupt and oppress others on a large and intolerable scale, then it is a religious obligation upon Muslims to attempt to unseat them, provided, of course, that their attempt stands a clear chance of success. As elsewhere in Islamic law, God gives people the right to go to hell, but not to take others with them.

Lest it be thought that contemporary Muslim activism envisages some kind of theocratic Fascism, let us remind ourselves that the practical institutions of the faith fall into

The Final Imperative

two categories. First, there are those matters which pertain to the individual religious life: prayer, fasting, pilgrimage and the like. Secondly, there are matters which regulate the life of the believing community and order it in a just fashion. The Islamic state, properly and traditionally constituted, does not interfere with the former, but seeks to regulate and reform only the latter category of actions. The fact that this distinction is not fully understood by some puritanical and 'extremist' groups of little Islamic education does not mean that the mainstream Islamic movement will institute inquisitions – whatever hostile journalists may maintain.

Islam's fight is against injustice. It does not seek to impose its beliefs by force. Any authentically Islamic order must recall that religious freedom is granted by the revealed Law, part of whose justification is precisely to secure the rights of minorities who also, to a greater or lesser extent, walk in the Lord's path.

Had it not been for God's repelling some men by [the Law, i.e. by] means of others, then cloisters and churches, oratories and mosques, in which God's name is abundantly mentioned, would assuredly have been destroyed.

(K 22:40)

6

Some readers may have wished for a less polemical essay, more relaxed in its attitudes and also perhaps in its conclusions. The attitudes may have seemed relentlessly accusatory, the concluding imperatives urgent and demanding. It is too late in the night for some kind of retrospective regret over the vehemence of my idiom. It is, in any case, part of a lengthy and deliberate indignation at modern Christians and liberals who often sit on the moral fence pretending that they have washed their hands clean of the political muck. The delinquencies of Muslim fanatics account for much of the news every evening and Christians and liberals only occasionally interfere in order to get rid

112

of the odd tyrant in the Third World. Well, that should settle it, they think. But the rebellious real world is not eager to support such self-righteousness. The standard Western critique of the Muslim involvement with power survives intellectually solely because its producers exploit the ignorance and prejudice of foreign and partisan audiences.

The realities of power in the real world all point an accusing finger at the ubiquitous West – at once secular in professed ambition yet proudly religious in the hour of moral justification and accountability. Questions of political humility are here unavoidable. It is wrong to see traditional Islam as a Fascist or totalitarian ideology with no resources for self-criticism or humility. Wrong indeed – unless one were, as in the case of many Western critics, defending a thesis at all costs.

In the last decade of the turbulent twentieth century, the political compass swings to its two new significant points: Islam and the West. The failure of American imperialism in Iran and the Russian disappointment in Afghanistan, both caused by Islam, jointly prepared the context for the end of the Cold War. The termination of that conflict, in any case a struggle within the European family, throws into sharp relief the tension between the Muslim East and the all-powerful West – which has now absorbed Russia, the failed superpower. The Berlin Wall has come down but Western ideologues are busy building an even higher wall between themselves and that old enemy from Arabia. Each brick of prejudice – one of which we have examined here – is being carefully laid in its place. The task for those of goodwill in both camps will be to dismantle this new wall and put an end to what has been called 'the war with the longest truce in history'.

Popular as well as sophisticated opinion in the West sees Islam as the new threat – and this despite the fact that the Muslim peoples today are plagued with war, famine, disunity and military weakness. Recent surveys show that Westerners have now transferred their fear of Russia on to Muslims: only 11 per cent in a 1990 *Times* survey saw

Russia as the main threat, while 49 per cent surmised that Islam was the enemy of the future. Again, it is no coincidence that the four most hated men in the world, according to American popular belief, are all Muslims – three Arabs and one Iranian. Not a Russian spy in sight!

Part of this Western hatred is inspired by what is seen as Muslim bloodlust and indiscriminate violence. Yet terrorism is itself the outcome of powerlessness and desperation. People normally embark on the road to violence when all other avenues are closed. 'Terrorism' by Muslims gives Westerners a conclusive reason for ending oppression, not a fragile excuse for perpetuating it.

In fact the modern Islamic revival has chosen to focus its energies on social works: health clinics, schools, orphanages and the like. This aspect of it is entirely veiled from consumers of the Western media, who only know the Islamic movement from some of its political manifestations. Baffled by its rhetoric, and incensed by the 'behaviour of a small minority of activists, Western public opinion views it as a force of aberrant evil which endangers the progress of 'modern' (a euphemism for 'Western') values. Christians must understand that this image is the precise opposite of the Muslim perception, which sees Westernization as the harbinger of cultural extinction and social breakdown, a malign cancer imposed by force, first by Christian and post-Christian armies, and later by military régimes presiding over a Muslim world whose indigenous political processes have been deconstructed by colonial policy, whose territory stands divided by national boundaries not drawn by Muslim hands, and where the still devout masses are held down by small Westernized élites with little but contempt for indigenous culture and values. It should be unsurprising that these masses are instinctively hostile to such an order.

There can be an enduring peace between Islam and the West, in the ideological (rather than the geographical) sense of the civilization created, through worldwide colonial exploitation, by the peoples of Europe. Certainly, Muslims are religiously obliged to seek a mandate for peace. But such a peace can only endure if Muslims are treated honourably, as equals, as heirs of an equally valid and worthy civilization. Islam is a faith, not a nuisance. Non-Muslims need to be careful with Islam and its adherents. But this is as much a plea for compassion as for caution. For Islam is to be both feared and revered. If not, the confrontation is both inevitable and necessary; Islamic revival will unquestionably mark the character of the coming millennium. A wounded Muslim humanity has been victimized long enough: in the first year of the Hot War, Muslims give notice that they wish to live with the West, not under it.

There is today, sadly, a continuous and deep psychic tension between the West and the decisive religion, Islam. It is evidenced on multiple levels – in the regularity with which the West interferes with Islamic destinies, the way in which 'scholars' co-operate with novelists in locating Muslim sites that satisfy a Western appetite for violence and sex. Somehow Muslims cannot be trusted to run their own societies; they need to be controlled and guided. It is the old orientalist agenda, brazen in its new confidence, shameless in its endorsement of double, even triple ethical standards. Thus, for example, the West has interpreted the Muslim response to Rushdie to be a Muslim threat to *Western* identity. Why else did it interfere in what is, at the end of the day, an internal fight between brothers, the rightly guided and the one who, in St Paul's idiom, 'walketh disorderly'? Again, the Iraqi invasion of Kuwait, while unjustified, might reasonably have been reversed by Arab diplomacy and long-term sanctions. The West's desire to interfere forcefully was motivated by personal interest – although we need not here disturb the complacency of those Anglican clergymen and Conservative British politicians who pretend that the Western involvement was motivated by moral principle. And God does not guide a perverse generation.

Christianity and Islam are usually identified as being the two imperial powers, so to speak, in the religious world. But in the clash between militant secularity and theistic faith, Western Christianity will be a minor player. For post-Enlightenment Christianity has now been beseiged by secularity for centuries. It is a largely spent religious force. Unsurprisingly, it has recently retreated more or less wholly into secluded obscurity, making Christian theism a cloistered religion, torn away from its historical roots, and set on the secular landscape of power and polity not as a landmark and a beacon but rather as an excrescence and a warning. It is as possible to admire the impulse to humility in modern Christian ideals of powerlessness as it is to deplore in these the will to abdication of colossal social responsibility in a world urgently in need of reform.

Islam is, of course, the significant entry in the competition. Japan's economic power might temporarily disturb Westerners, but money without a challenging ideology can safely be ignored. Islam cannot be ignored: the Arabs might run out of oil and cash, but they seem unlikely to run out of Islam. In any case, the authentic Muslims' anti-colonialist radicalism secretly impresses and then depresses Western minds committed to upholding their own interests in Islamic lands under the pretext of peace and philanthropy.

Islam, a unified enterprise of faith and power, a sincere militancy that seeks to secure justice, has already thwarted the expansionist ambitions of two superpowers in this century. The religion of Muhammad stands proudly on the blood-stained landscape, the muezzin calling the faithful to peace and prayer in the midst of Israeli bullets. (How decisive a religion!) Islam's almost miraculous durability as a political variable in every Middle Eastern power calculation has baffled and angered Western orientalist expertise which seeks to understand this strange religion without exercising the least sympathy with its adherents. In any case, orientalism is now recognized to be both irreverent and irrelevant. In the meantime, Muslims remain confident, despite intelligent and profound animus from all disbelieving quarters, of the signal triumph of divine purpose over all rebellious wills and federations that seek to undermine Islam and, paradoxically, their own best interests.

Islam's professed involvement with power is a declaration of a wish to establish the divine kingdom on earth. By God's grace – naturally.

The last word, of course, is about peace. 'O you who believe', says the Koran, 'enter fully into a state of peace' (Koran 2:208). This is an imperative, the final imperative. For the pursuit of peace is an active affair. A wholesome and enduring peace, founded on justice and mercy, is not easy to secure in our kind of world – a world in which, in the greatest yet most challenging paradox, one often needs to wage war in order to secure a hearing for peace.

DATE DUE

NOV 2 8 2007			

HIGHSMITH 45-220